Dominiek Dendoove\

translated by Ian Connerty

– Ypres as Holy Ground –

MENIN GATE
& LAST POST

de
klaproos

This book is dedicated to Gustav-Adam Dendooven,
who was born during its preparation.

© De Klaproos Editions, Hostenstraat 4, 8670 Koksijde, Belgium

D/2001/6526/4
ISBN 90-5508-051-9

Edited and sold by De Klaproos Editions, info@klaproos.be
Website: www.klaproos.be

First published on 31 October 2001 (day of the 25.000th Last Post)
Second edition April 2003

Contents

Foreword

Of all the memorials to the missing constructed by the Commonwealth War Graves Commission after the two world wars, the Menin Gate has perhaps captured the public's affection and interest more than any other.

It has done so because, even 75 years after it was unveiled, it remains a living memorial, not only to those who died in the battlefields around Ypres, but for all those Commonwealth servicemen and women who died in two world wars, no matter where they are buried or commemorated. It stands proudly in defiance of the elements and of the oblivion of time, a daily reminder of the events which unfolded here from 1914 to 1918 and of the 54,000 men and women who passed this way, never to return. Their names represent tens of thousands of families, comrades and friends throughout the Commonwealth who received the tragic news that their son, brother, father or friend was "missing, believed killed". To them and their succeeding generations, the Menin Gate provides comfort, a place to visit and remember because, to borrow from Field Marshall Lord Plumer's speech when the Gate was unveiled in July 1927, "He is not missing. He is here."

The memorial is a reflection in stone of the determination we all share never to forget those who died. It is also a living symbol of the spirit and bond of friendship between the Commonwealth nations and the Belgian people. A friendship that manifests itself in that nightly act of remembrance, the sounding of the Last Post. That simple and dignified ceremony, deeply stirs the emotions, memory and imagination of all who hear it. May it long continue.

It gives me great pleasure, therefore, to contribute to a publication which aims to explain the history and reasoning behind the memorial's creation and the Commission's efforts to maintain it. It is my hope that this book will answer your questions about the memorial and encourage even greater numbers to pay their respects to those commemorated on its walls.

To view the row upon row of names at the memorial, or indeed at any of the Commonwealth's war cemeteries and memorials world wide, is a moving experience, but we must never believe it is one without hope. As the final notes of the Last Post echo around this hallowed arch each night, the Commission and those witnesses to this nightly act of remembrance stiffen their resolve to carry the names we have read in our hearts and minds, conscious of their sacrifice and sharing the same commitment to a free and peaceful world.

Richard Kellaway
Director-General
Commonwealth War Graves Commission

"This is Holy Ground!"

British plans for the city of Ypres after the First World War

With the possible exception of the Cloth Hall[1], the Menin Gate Memorial is the most famous building in modern-day Ypres – due in no small part to the daily playing of the Last Post Ceremony under its massive stone arches. The Menin Gate is known far and wide as the single most important contribution made by the British people to the reconstruction of Ypres after the Great War. Equally, the Gate is regarded by many as the most important British war memorial in the world.

Yet for all its fame, few people realise that the present-day monument was the result of conflicting visions and a complex – and often difficult – creative process.

To re-build or not to re-build? an international debate

Even before the end of the war, the possible re-building of the Cloth Hall and St Martin's Cathedral was a subject of much heated debate. The supporters of re-building were divided into two broad camps: the "traditionalists", who favoured complete and identical reconstruction in the original style, and the "modernists", who wished to create something new and exciting.

In Belgium, the "traditionalist" group was lead by the Burgomaster (Mayor) of Ypres, René Colaert, and the City Architect, Jules Coomans. Their preference was for an integral reconstruction of the city, including exact replicas of the most famous pre-1914 historical buildings, a view in

Jules Coomans (1871-1937),
City Architect of Ypres.
(COLLECTION JEAN COOMANS)

9

'Halles d'Ypres - Projet du Beffroi', coloured
pen and ink drawing by Jules Coomans,
3 May 1916. (COLLECTION JEAN COOMANS)

which they were supported by Minister Joris
Helleputte. Colaert and Coomans had both
been forced to flee to France during the early
years of the war. Even so, their numerous
speeches and publications on the issue of "reconstruction" received considerable attention
in Great Britain and the Netherlands.

In this latter country, the modernist Bruges
architect, Huib Hoste, organised a survey
amongst his fellow-colleagues on this same
subject. In 1918, he wrote to 57 architects and
artists and to 11 cultural-historical organisations, requesting their opinions with regard
to the re-building of the Cloth Hall.

Some of the answers were surprising, not least
from Piet Mondriaan, one of Holland's most
famous and most respected 20th century artists.
He wrote: "Whilst I am in favour of all that is
new, it seems to me that in this particular case
aesthetic, cultural-historical, national and
international considerations all argue in favour
of an exact reconstruction…"[2]

More predictable, perhaps, were the replies
received from architects De Klerk, Dudok and
Berlage and from the multi-talented "De
Stijl" artist and theorist, Theo van Doesburg.
They all categorically rejected the idea of
historical replicas. Others wished to preserve certain elements of the ruins
within a city re-built in the modern style. A further group wished to break
with the past completely, to use the tabula rasa created by the war to
sweep away the ruins and replace them with a modernist experiment.

As for Huib Hoste himself, he would probably have agreed with the comments of Eugène Dhuicque, a celebrated Belgian designer and professor of
medieval architecture, who wrote in 1919 that the ruins of the Cloth Hall,
St Martin's Cathedral and the surrounding houses should be preserved in
a memorial park, thereby creating what he called "a zone of silence".

Whilst highlighting these "professional" opinions, it must also be remembered that the reconstruction debate was not only of interest to architects, academics and government officials. The same arguments were discussed in the mass-circulation newspapers and periodicals of the day and even several diaries of quite "humble" origin make mention of the reconstruction issue.[3]

Ypres as "holy ground" for the British

It is self-evident that the whole question of the re-building of Ypres was a particularly sensitive and emotive one for the peoples of Great Britain and her Empire. British troops had been present in Ypres from the very beginning to the very end of the war. After the evacuation of the last civilians in 1915, they had been virtually masters of the city for four long and dreadful years. By 1918, more than 200,000 of their fellow country-

The centre of Ypres, as seen from the ramparts, *February 1919*. (IFF DOCUMENT CENTRE)

men lay dead or missing in the grim fields of "the immortal Salient". For those who survived, their lives would be marked forever by the memories of their terrible experiences in "Wipers". For all these reasons, in the eyes of British public opinion the city of Ypres was more than just a symbol. As early as 1916, the Canadian author and officer, Beckles Willson, had formulated what came to be the standard British perception of Ypres: "It is only a heap of ruins, but it is an eternal memorial of British valour. It is only a shell-swept graveyard, but the graves are those of our heroic dead."[4]

In these circumstances, it is hardly surprising that the poignant phrase "holy ground" should eventually come to be applied to the city. In many British papers the ruins of Ypres were deemed to be of equal, if not greater, significance than the ruins of Pompei. Writing in his book *Ypres – the Holy Ground of British Arms*, which was published early in 1920, Beckles Willson commented that for the families of those who had lost loved ones, Ypres had become the equivalent of what Jerusalem is for the Jewish people and what Mecca is for the Muslims.[5]

This contention that Ypres must be regarded as "holy ground" was also taken up by a number of prominent public figures in Belgium. Not least amongst these was King Albert I, who during a speech to mark the award of the British Military Cross to the city (on 19 May 1920) declared that Ypres was "sacred ground".[6]

Churchill and his wish to buy the ruins

In view of the fact that British public opinion viewed the battlefields of the Ypres Salient in these almost semi-mystical terms, it was perhaps inevitable that at some stage the British government would seek to demand a say in the planning for the future of the city. As early as September 1918 the new Imperial War Graves Commission was active in Ypres, supervising the construction and maintenance of military cemeteries and memorials. It would be through this organisation that the British would primarily seek to assert their influence.[7] The Commission's counterpart – and counterweight – in the Belgian official hierarchy was "de Dienst der Verwoeste Gewesten" (the Department for the Devastated Zone), an offshoot of the Ministry of the Interior.

Sir Reginald Blomfield, architect of the Menin Gate

Sir Reginald Blomfield, *circa 1920*.

When viewed in purely architectural terms, the career of Reginald Blomfield has rather fallen into the shadows in recent years, particularly in comparison with his fellow senior architects in the Imperial War Graves Commission: Baker, Lutyens and Holden. Nevertheless, during his own day Blomfield stood at the very top of his profession.

Reginald Blomfield was born into a largely clerical family on 20 December 1856. He studied at Exeter and Oxford and in 1881 went to work for his uncle, Arthur Blomfield, who was well-known for his work in the field of ecclesiastical architecture. In 1884, Reginald set up on his own. He felt little empathy with the then-current popularity for the Neo-Gothic style and was in favour of a return to the classical and renaissance traditions. Even so, much of the work from his early years can still be placed firmly within the "Arts and Crafts" movement. Later on, Blomfield (like so many of his contemporaries) would acquire a reputation for his work on country mansions for the landed gentry. Here he could give freer expression to his preference for classical forms, as practised by the great British architects of the 17th century: Inigo Jones and Christopher Wren. As far as landscape and garden design were concerned, Blomfield again advocated a return to the formal and the traditional.

Throughout his life, Blomfield continued to write a number of theoretical works on architecture – works in which he was not afraid to confront the polemical issues of his day. The titles of his most well-known books all betray his architectural leanings: *The Formal Garden in England* (1892), *A History of Renaissance Architecture in England,*

1500-1900 (1897), *The Mistress Art* (1908) and *A History of French Architecture, 1661-1774* (1911-1912). By virtue of these books, Blomfield lay at the basis of the classical revival in English architecture, which began around the turn of the century: a revival sometimes known as the "Wrennaissance", after the great 17th century architect.

In 1906, Blomfield was appointed as a professor of architecture at the prestigious Royal Academy. In 1912 he became Chairman of the RIBA (Royal Institute of British Architects) and in 1914 he was elected to full membership of the Royal Academy – one of only three architects at that time to be awarded such an honour.

Blomfield's most famous designs include: Lady Margaret Hall in Oxford (1896-1929); the public library and water tower in Lincoln (ca. 1900 & 1910); The United University Club in London's Pall Mall (1924); the Quadrant, linking Piccadilly and Regent Street (1923-27); The Headrow in Leeds (1926-1936); and Lambeth Bridge in London (1932).

The First World War gave a considerable boost to Blomfield's reputation and career. Before the war his work was only known to his fellow architects and the restricted circles of the rich and famous. After the war, his worked would be opened to a much wider public – not in the least by his designs for various war cemeteries and memorials. His name began to appear more and more frequently in the press and in 1919 he was knighted.

During the inter-war period Blomfield developed into a strong – perhaps the main – opponent of all that was modern in British architecture: what he called "Modernismus", "so as to stress its alien, Teutonic character." For Blomfield, good architecture must always strive to achieve a correct balance between form and function. For this reason, he continued to point to the French classical tradition as a source of inspiration: "What is really important in modern architecture is the relation between these two almost antagonistic tendencies (classical-romantic). In the old French classical tradition we find a definite reach for beauty of form for its own sake, for symmetry, rhythm, harmony and proportion, even sometimes at the expense of immediate efficiency." [73]

As a person, Blomfield comes across to us as a strong, almost dictatorial man, for whom architecture is the greatest good. He appears as a typical product of the British establishment of the time: patriotic, elegant, always striving to reach some higher goal. His controversial comments are legion. Not only was he disparaging of all modern architecture, but foreigners also received the full force of his pen and tongue. Of the French and their attitude toward British cemeteries he wrote: "The French are chary of compliments to anybody but themselves, and they may feel reluctant to say anything, as their own municipal cemeteries are a disgrace to civilisation."[74] Nor did the Belgians escape the Blomfield treatment. He pressed strongly for a permanent caretaker at the Menin Gate, "otherwise 'More Belgarum' the place will be treated like a latrine."[75] However, Blomfield's criticisms were by no means egocentric. He was equally happy to give praise, where praise was due. In this context, for example, he was full of admiration for the work of the Belgian craftsmen on the Menin Gate.

After his death, on 28 December 1942, Reginald Blomfield was written off by many young architects – not without some justification – as being the main proponent of all that was reactionary and stifling in British architecture. It is certainly true that in comparison with his contemporary, Edwin Lutyens, his designs show little originality, but it may still yet transpire that modern indifference to much of his work is both premature and misplaced.

Blomfield's work for the Imperial War Graves Commission

After the previous appointments of Herbert Baker and Edwin Lutyens, at the beginning of 1918 the Imperial War Graves Commission also approached Reginald Blomfield to become one of its Senior Architects. Blomfield agreed and resigned his commission as a lieutenant in the London Regiment. Consequently, he never knew the realities of war, but remained permanently on the home front. His two sons did, however, see active service: the oldest in India and the youngest (Austin, his later successor) as a territorial near Ypres.

No easy task lay before the architects of the Imperial War Graves Commission. It was their sorry duty to give concrete expression, in clear but symbolically charged forms, to the grief of an entire nation. Of the three (later four) Senior Architects, Blomfield was the most conventional and patriotic: the establishment man. Even so, he fully supported the Commission's basic principle that every dead or missing soldier should be commemorated individually and equally, irrespective of rank, social standing and religion. In his cemeteries – many of which are to be found in the Ypres Salient – he tried to create geometrically idealised gardens in the French style. As a result, these cemeteries are seldom eye-catching, and have even been described as "uninspired" – a fact in part attributable to his heavy reliance on assistant architects in many of his more minor IWGC projects.[76] It was for the benefit of such young assistant architects that Blomfield wrote a series of guidelines in a memorandum dated September 1918. The first paragraphs of this memorandum quickly reveal Blomfield's own personal philosophy for the commemoration of the fallen. All designs for the cemeteries must fulfil two fundamental criteria: firstly, they must provide a fitting memorial for those who died in this most terrible of wars; secondly, they must seek to give abstract expression to the ideas of heroic self-sacrifice in a noble cause. The aims must be achieved through the use of simple and sober forms, with no undue emphasis on sentiment or architectural frills. He advised his young colleagues to seek their inspiration in the work of Vauban, the great French military engineer, about whom he had written a biography. (In this respect, the very least that can be said of Blomfield is that he practised what he preached: all these same basic principles would later be used for his own design of the Menin Gate.)

In all, Blomfield drew plans for 120 IWGC cemeteries, more than 40 of which are in the Ypres Salient. Amongst the most well-known are Lijssenthoek, New Irish Farm, Poperinghe New and Ramparts Cemetery.

In every British military cemetery, there stands a Cross of Sacrifice: a relatively modern, sober and timeless piece of architecture. This cross was also Blomfield's work but its introduction was not without difficulties. The Cross at Boulogne Eastern Cemetery split down the middle during a storm soon after its erection, forcing Blomfield to alter its design and make it significantly stronger.

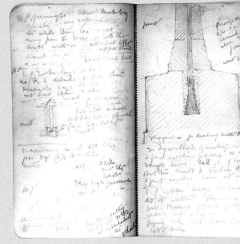

Blomfield's notes for the Cross of Sacrifice at Lijssenthoek Military Cemetery. (RIBA, LONDON)

This same Cross was also frequently used for "civic" war memorials in Great Britain, but in addition Blomfield was also asked to design a number of "one-off" monuments. Two of the most important of these stand on the north bank of the River Thames in London. The Belgian war memorial in Embankment Gardens comprises a statue by the Belgian sculptor, Victor Rousseau, enclosed by Blomfield's semi-circular structure in Portland stone. The R.A.F. Memorial consists of a pillar surmounted by a globe, on which a splendid gilt eagle sits perched. The eagle was the work of William Reid Dick, who would later sculpt the lion for the Menin Gate.

In contrast to these British monuments, where the location was pre-determined, in 1919 Blomfield had almost free choice of site for the location of the great British war memorial in Ypres. His eventually decision in favour of the gateway through the ramparts constructed by his old idol, Vauban, was architecturally shrewd and contributed in no small measure to the impressive qualities of the finished monument. In retrospect, it is curious that Blomfield should have been chosen for the Menin Gate project at all. The Imperial War Graves Commission had reasoned that Blomfield's personal aesthetic preferences would be better suited than those of the more modern Lutyens to this provincial Flemish town, "with all its Gothic associations". Yet Blomfield had been a life-long opponent of everything to do with the Gothic movement!
Equally curious were his good relations with Jules Coomans, the City Architect in Ypres, who is widely recognised as one of the last great exponents of the Neo-Gothic style in Belgium.

The Menin Gate gave Blomfield the opportunity to put all his architectural ideas into practice on a grand scale. During a three-day visit in 1919, he had studied the site from all angles and had already formed a first impression of how the memorial should look (an impression from which the finished monument varies very little). Blomfield was not ashamed to draw his inspiration from the work of others and once again he turned to the oeuvre of his hero, Marquis Sébastien de Vauban. His ideas for the Menin Gate were based closely on Vauban's Porte de la Citadelle, a brick-vaulted passageway over a main road into the French city of Nancy, which had been demolished some decades before. The Porte de la Citadelle had crossed its roadway in a single elliptical span, illuminated by a series of roundels let into the apex of the arch. This drew Blomfield towards the concept of a similar single span over the roadway and footpath under the Menin Gate. He rejected a suggestion from his colleague, Aston Webb, that a colonnade of pillars should be erected along the entire length of the central Hall of Memory: these columns would destroy the carefully-balanced proportions of the design and would block the fall of light onto the name panels. Blomfield's own plans for the creation of an open plaza on the far side of the bridge (where the Frenchlaan now stands) and for a through-view from the Menin Gate to the Cloth Hall both stranded on what he called "the indomitable proprietary instincts of the Belgians."[77]

"La Porte de la Citadelle" in Nancy (19th century engraving): Blomfield's inspiration for the Menin Gate. (BIBLIOTHÈQUE MUNICIPALE, NANCY)

Blomfield had originally intended that the vaulting in the Menin Gate should be made from brick. Fortunately, one of his engineers pointed out that brick would be more likely to absorb light than to reflect it, which could severely reduce the legibility of the name panels. Blomfield quickly appreciated the wisdom of this argument and switched to a design based on a coffer-vaulting in reinforced concrete. This was not only aesthetically more attractive but also resulted in better acoustics, since the coffers more efficiently broke up any echo effect. For the outward appearance of his monument, Blomfield resorted to the forms of classical antiquity: Doric columns, cornices, symbolic trophies. Nevertheless, the requirements of form were strictly subjugated to the requirements of content: central to the whole concept were the all-important name panels. This is the great strength of Blomfield's design: without sentiment (but perhaps not entirely free from bombast), the monument makes perfectly clear what its purpose is: to commemorate the dead. Notwithstanding the texts "Pro Patria" and "Pro Rege" on the facade, the Menin Gate does not seek to glorify war and is in no way intended as a monument to victory. It is a monument of remembrance, which seeks to underline in stone the terrible scale of the bloodletting which took place during the First World War: a giant shrine for 55,000 soldiers who died in the fields around Ypres and who have no known grave.

In his memoirs, which appeared in 1932, Blomfield wrote that the Menin Gate was the only one of his designs with which he was completely satisfied: even given the chance, he would change nothing. "If I am ever remembered, I hope it may be by the Menin Gate, my design for the completion of the Quadrant and Lambeth Bridge."[78] He was destined to get his wish, for his name will always be most closely associated with his most famous creation: the British memorial to the missing in Ypres - the Menin Gate.

The British made their first move shortly after the Armistice. On 21 January 1919 the Governing Body of the Imperial War Graves Commission met for the eighth time. The Chairman was Winston Churchill, in his capacity as Secretary of State for War. Halfway through the meeting, Churchill unexpectedly made the following proposal: "I think I should mention to the Commission at this moment the very strong wish I have myself in this matter. I should like us to acquire the whole of the ruins of Ypres. I do not know how many of the members round the table have visited Ypres, but a more beautiful monument than Ypres in the afternoon light can hardly be conceived. A more sacred place for the British race does not exist in the world. Around that battlefield probably more than 300,000 of our men of the British Army are buried, and if there is any one place in the whole world which is associated with our race it is that. Would it not be possible to acquire Ypres, either by a gift from the Belgians or by some arrangement, by purchase or some arrangement, as British property, and gather there round these ruins and make it the centre of all the burying places around, and put up memorials there of an approved pattern in accordance with what would beautify and would not impair the scene. It would show the names of everyone who had fallen on all that great series of battle fields radiating from Ypres. No attempt to reconstitute agriculture or industry on this area should be allowed; it should be left entirely as a garden, and as a burial place, with flowers and plants and so forth. Then hostels could be put up and arrangements made for the people who wished to visit the graves in the burial grounds. At any rate I think it is worth thinking of. It is quite true it would not last more than three or four hundred years but it would last as long as that and it would become a very great place of pilgrimage for the descendants of all those who had taken part in defending Ypres against all attacks…"[8]

In the discussions following this announcement, Fabian Ware, the strong man of the Commission, proposed that a definite decision should be postponed until the following meeting, in order to allow time to contact the Belgian authorities and gauge their initial reaction.

It is not clear how the British press got wind of this proposal, but on 1 February 1919 a telling advertisement appeared in the *Times*. The advertisement was a request for ground for sale along the Menin Road (i.e. outside the city), since the Belgian government was planning to leave the ruins of Ypres in tact.

A British soldier on sentry duty in the ruins of Ypres. (IWM, London)

CHAIRMAN: I think it would be a good thing   I think I should mention
to the Commission at this moment the very strong wish I have myself
in this matter. I should like us to acquire the whole of the ruins
of Ypres. I do not know how many of the members round the table
have visited Ypres, but a more beautiful monument than Ypres in
the afternoon light can hardly be conceived. A more sacred place
for the British race does not exist in the world. Around that
battlefield probably more than 300,000 of our men of the British
Army are buried, and if there is any one place in the whole world

Churchill's famous quote, *21 January 1919*. (CWGC, Maidenhead)

The papers of the Imperial War Graves Commission make it clear that not everyone considered Churchill's proposal to be realistic. At least one official commented that the Belgians might wish to retain the ruins as a monument to their own war dead. Other Commissioners were more enthusiastic. Alfred Mond, Director of the Office of Public Works, informed Churchill that he was 100% behind the idea and that he would do all that he could to "consolidate" the ruins. This was necessary (at least according to Mond), since it appeared that the Belgians were doing little or nothing to protect or preserve the shattered remains of Ypres.[9] For this and many other reasons, the impulsive Churchill was anxious to get matters settled as quickly as possible. On 24 February 1919 he demanded (in his own inimitable and imperious style) to know what action Ware had already taken to bring about his wishes. Having done very little, the Director (and Vice-Chairman) of the Commission immediately dispatched a senior official to Brussels, to discuss the matter with the British Ambassador. At the same time, he attempted to temper Churchill's enthusiasm by pointing out to the Minister of War the huge range of potential problems that the purchase of the ruins would entail. As a tactical move, he also suggested that Churchill should be appointed as an honorary member of the Anglo-Belgian Committee, which supervised the implementation of the bilateral agreement on war graves. After all, argued Ware, this was where the real battle over the ruins of Ypres would eventually be fought.[10]

Impatient as ever, on 16 March 1919 Churchill again stated his arguments in favour of acquiring the ruins: it would allow consideration to be given to the many requests from individuals for the erection of private memorials; it would allow consideration to be given to the many requests from military units for the erection of regimental memorials; it would preserve a historically important battleground.[11]

Yet for all Churchill's haste, in his very first report the Commission's man in Brussels made it clear that it was likely to be some time before the Belgian government was ready to take any final decision on Ypres. Notwithstanding growing pressure from the former inhabitants, who wished to rebuild their old houses in their original locations, the regime was currently considering a proposal to rebuild on a new site to the north of the city. There were also a number of other options, which needed to be assessed carefully. One of these was a proposal by a senior member of the Belgian nobility, Count Goblet d'Alviella. The Count suggested that the Cloth Hall, the Cathedral and their surrounding houses should be left in ruins; that the area between the ruins and the Minneplein should be cleared; and that the Minneplein itself should be transformed into a giant international cemetery, with the ruined city as a backdrop.[12]

The fact that various schemes of this kind were still under serious consideration in Belgium, allowed Fabian Ware to persuade Churchill that the most sensible policy for the British government at this juncture was one of "wait and see". Consequently, it

Reservoir North Cemetery, a British military cemetery on the Minneplein, *1919.*
In the background stand the ruins of St Martin's Cathedral and the Cloth Hall.

was agreed that further information should be gathered but that no action should be taken until the Belgian parliament had settled the question of damage compensation for its own citizens.[13]

In retrospect, it now seems clear that Ware's non-committal position was an attempt to play for time, whilst he tried to find ways to escape from – or, at the very least, reduce – Churchill's stifling influence. His attempts to refer the whole Ypres question to the recently established Anglo-Belgian Committee can also be seen in this light.[14] Sadly, the reports of this committee are no longer available, so that it is impossible to know whether or not Churchill's purchase proposal was ever discussed. Moreover, for various reasons, Churchill was unable to attend the next six meetings of the War Graves Commission. Slowly but surely, Ware was gaining the upper hand and the Minister of War's grandiose plans for Ypres began to fade more and more into the background.

The Menin Gate before 1914 [85]

The Hangwaert Gate on the city plan drawn up by Thévelin and Destrée in *1564.*

Growing population and increasing trade led to the foundation of a settlement at Ypres during the 10th century. The embryonic city had its own system of defences, based on natural watercourses and a series of earthworks. On the eastern side of this system – where the Menin Gate now stands – these defences followed more or less the line of the present-day ramparts.

It is not known with any degree of certainty when the first gateway through these earthen defence works was constructed, but it was probably around 1214, when a protective moat was dug along the eastern side of the city. During the Middle Ages this gate – which was later to become the Menin Gate – was known as the Hangwaert Gate: literally, the gate leading to the gallows field.

During the 13th century, the city continued to expand and by 1260 had a population of some 40,000 souls. This made Ypres one of the largest and most important cities in Europe. Sheer weight of numbers led to the growth of the settlement beyond its original defensive walls and in 1303 the resulting suburbs were enclosed within a new earthwork, known as the "Uuterste veste" or Outer Rampart. In 1383 the city's new defences were put to the test (by of all people) ... the English. Under the leadership of Henry Spencer, Bishop of Norwich, an English army, supported by levies from the rival city of Ghent, laid siege to Ypres for a period of two months. Having failed to starve the defenders into sub-mission, the besiegers attempted to take the city by storm. On 8 August they attacked first one city gate and then another, including the Hangwaert Gate. According to tradition, only the miraculous intervention of Our Lady enabled the brave defenders to keep the English at bay, but the siege was broken and Bishop Henry withdrew to Calais – a divinely inspired victory which is still celebrated on the first Sunday of August each year. The Siege of Ypres had led to the destruction of the outlying suburbs – they were never rebuilt – and had shown the necessity of constructing stone walls to defend the city. This process was quickly undertaken and the Hangwaert Gate was rebuilt in stone around 1395. Unfortunately, the golden years for the city had passed and both its prosperity and its population went into a gradual but irreversible decline. By 1491, the once proud metropolis had been reduced to a mere 7,600 inhabitants. During this period of economic crisis, the Hangwaert Gate was bricked up, probably in 1480. By 1564, however, the gate had been reinstated, (as evidenced by its inclusion in the city plan drawn up in that same year by Thévelin and Destrée). The new gate was not designed to provide access to and from the city, but gave out onto a defensive island in the moat. In view of its war-like function, the new two-storey structure was foreseen with battlements and embrasures.

During the 17th century the Hangwaert Gate received a new name: the Antwerp Gate. Based on a map of Ypres contained in Sanderus' famous 1640 book *Flandria Illustrata*, it seems clear that the so-called "gate" was still little more than a sally-port onto the defensive island constructed the century before.

Shortly thereafter, however, a bridge over the moat was rebuilt. The Spaniards – of whose empire the Low Countries now formed a part – were keen to adopt the city's defences to the requirements of modern artillery. Consequently, in 1669 they built a new fortification – known as the Citadel – on the far side of the moat, slightly to the south-east of the Antwerp Gate, which itself was once again closed up. The expansion of France under Louis XIV led to the capture of Ypres in 1678, following which the city became part of the defensive chain protecting the Sun King's northern flank. The famous military engineer, Sébastien Le Prestre de Vauban, drastically modernised and expanded the existing rampart complex. The bridge at the Antwerp Gate was reinstated and the Gate itself received an imposing classical facade,

The Antwerp Gate post *1678*.

25

complete with Doric columns and a decorative relief of Louis' coat of arms.

After 35 years of French occupation, the Peace of Utrecht (1713) placed Ypres under Austrian rule. By this time, the city's defences were no longer as important as they had once been and in 1782 Emperor Joseph II decreed that they should be demolished. The invasion of the French Revolutionary Army in 1792 temporarily changed this situation, but following the defeat of Napoleon and the creation of the United Provinces, the ramparts were gradually decommissioned, thereby acquiring their present-day appearance. During the period 1804-1815 the Antwerp Gate had been renamed the Napoleon Gate, but after the Little Emperor's defeat at Waterloo the name was definitively changed to the Menin Gate – a not illogical choice, in view of the fact that the gate linked the Menin Street with the Menin Road, which in turn led on to the town of Menin, some 20 kilometres distant.

Following the creation of an independent Belgium in 1830, the ramparts lost whatever strategic significance they had once possessed and in 1852 the section to the north of the city was removed. By now, the Menin Gate had become little more than a covered passageway, some 20 metres long and just 3 metres wide. Because it was a constant hindrance to

The Menin Gate in *1904*. (FOTO DUHAMEEUW)

The Menin Gate *before 1914*.

In *1919* the well-known Ypres artist, Louis Titz, photographed his sons, Marcel and Paul, at the Menin Gate. Note the narrow gauge railway on the right.

26

traffic passing into and out of the eastern side of the city, in 1862 it was decided to demolish the passage and replace it with 13 metre-wide causeway across the Citadel Moat. As a finishing touch, two impressive stone lions were placed on either side of the road and thus the new Menin Gate – so famous to the British Army during the Great War – came into being.

British aerial photograph of the Menin Gate in the First World War.

The Menin Gate on *22 April 1915*, just a few hours before the German gas attack at the start of the Second Battle of Ypres. Chief of Police Pierre Vandenbraambussche (right) inspects the water pumps at the Menin Gate. These pumps were installed in the winter of 1914 to provide (none too clean) water to those citizens who had chosen to remain in the city. (FOTO ANTONY D'YPRES)

Beckles Willson and his ideas [15]

One of the first refugees to return, accompanied by some military men in front of the ruins of the Cloth Hall.

Life in Ypres in 1919 was far from normal. The war was over, but the city was still occupied by British troops and considerable power was still vested in the hands of a British Town Major. At the same time, more and more civilians were returning from abroad and the Mayor and the City Council had also arrived back to resume their old functions. This unusual state of affairs was bound to lead to misunderstandings at some stage, particularly given the emotional significance of Ypres for the British.

This delicate situation was not helped by the curious activities of the previously mentioned Canadian officer, Lieutenant-Colonel Beckles Willson.

Beckles Willson was prepared to repeat his singular and somewhat strident views to just about anyone who would listen and he did so at length in public meetings, in press articles and in his own publications. He was firmly convinced that the city must be kept in ruins, as a permanent setting for an immense British national cemetery: "A great marble chapel and sanctuary should be built opposite the Cloth Hall in the Grand'Place. Each Division in the British Army could have its own spacious plot – the Guards in the shadow of St Jacques – the troops who stemmed the tide in October 1914, overlooked by the high, ancient fragment of St Peter's. The cemeteries of the first Seven Divisions would range along the streets by the eastern Menin Gate, whose cobblestones are worn by the tramp during those four years of our infantry and the restless wheels of our guns."[16]

In 1919 Beckles Willson was acting as Town Major in Ypres. During his period of office he did all in his power to try and transform his ideas into reality. In his diary, Deacon Delaere wrote: "Mr. Beckles-Wilson (sic) has forbidden the repair or the re-building of houses in the city and has done everything he can to make the situation as difficult as possible for as long as possible."[17] In his memoirs the Canadian attempted to paint a rather different picture. His recollection was that a majority of the local citizens – including Deacon Delaere – were actually in favour of re-building the city at a new location: it was only Burgomaster Colaert, who stubbornly held out against this sensible idea![18] Convinced of the rightness of his cause, Beckles Willson lobbied the British Ambassador in Brussels and the Belgian Minister of Foreign Affairs, de Broqueville, for support. As if this was not enough, in November 1919 he began a lecture tour, which took him to no fewer than 66 venues in London and other major cities in Great Britain. The first of these lectures was attended by the Prince of Wales and was given wide coverage in several British and Belgian newspapers. Beckles Willson's meetings with veterans during his tour would subsequently lead to the foundation of the Ypres League in 1920.[19]

Given his views about the future of the city, it was only to be expected that the mushrooming of temporary barracks amongst the ruins would be a source of irritation for Beckles Willson. He was particularly upset by the use of these barracks as hotels, cafés or restaurants. On 5 July 1919 he wrote to Minister de Broqueville: "Nevertheless, unless steps are at once taken the Grand'Place as a shrine for universal pilgrimage will be ruined. Even as I write, six new huts are in process of erection – all estaminets. One, which is painted sky-blue, boldly calls itself "The British Tavern", which exposes us daily to the rebuke of Belgian and French visitors, who think we are responsible. The proprietor is a cabaretier from Brussels."[20]

Several weeks earlier, the headquarters of the British Fifth Zone – the zone including Ypres – had also written to the Ministry of War, stating that in return for its consolidation work on the ruins, it expected that these cheap and "vulgar" barracks would be removed.

The "British Tavern", which so annoyed Beckles Willson. Painted sky blue, it stood not far from the corner of the D'Hondtstraat and the Market Square.

Battlefield tourists, war-widows and British soldiers on a terrace in Ypres, *1919*. Note the members of the Indian Labour Corps in the background.

In a similar vein, a number of British papers (including the *Times* and the *Daily Chronicle*) gave considerable attention throughout 1919 to what they described as the "sacrilege" being perpetrated by the organisers of large-scale battlefield tourism.

Following consultations with his superior officer, Colonel A.O. Vaughan, Beckles Willson had notices placed on all the most important ruins in Ypres. These notices read: "This is Holy Ground! No stone of this fabric to be taken away. It is a heritage for all civilised people."[21]

In retrospect, it would appear that Beckles Willson was often acting on his own initiative, using his standard tactics of high-handedness and sheer bluff. Typical of his modus operandi was his "official" application in May 1919 to the Department for the Devastated Zone – supposedly on behalf of the Canadian government – for the use of several plots of land to the south and west of the Menin Gate (i.e. along the Bollingstraat and on the Ramparts). Admittedly, he had already tentatively discussed his ideas for this ground with the Canadian Prime Minister, Borden, and his proposals had been published in one of Canada's leading newspapers.[22] Beyond this, however, there was no formal support of any kind for his extravagant plans. According to these plans, a Canadian memorial would be built on the Bollingstraat, in the form of a museum or library, whilst the trenches and dug-outs along the Ramparts would be incorporated into a historical park. As Burgomaster Colaert had also apparently been persuaded to agree with Beckles Willson's scheme, Minister of Foreign Affairs de Broqueville gave his personal approval for the project to proceed. By September 1919, a smart new bungalow had appeared on the Ramparts (built with the help of German prisoners-of-war). This luxury barrack not only housed a Canadian information centre, but also provided accommodation for the Town Major – none other than Beckles Willson himself!

Town Major Beckles Willson welcomes an important visitor in his barrack on the ramparts near the Menin Gate, *1919*. (From BECKLES WILLSON, FROM QUEBEC TO PICCADILLY AND OTHER PLACES)

The new building was the subject of a question in the Belgian House of Representatives on 11 September 1919, when Representative Nolf asked if the government could confirm whether or not it was still planning to hand over this plot of land to the Canadian authorities.

The site near the Menin Gate that Beckles Willson had 'reserved' for the Canadian government, *1919*. (From BECKLES WILLSON, FROM QUEBEC TO PICCADILLY AND OTHER PLACES)

Shortly thereafter, the scheme also received considerable attention in Great Britain, following a frontpage article in the *Daily Express* on 23 September 1919. This was to be the undoing of the good Lieutenant-

Beckles Willson's information office on the ramparts, near the Menin Gate. The ramparts are viewed from outside the city, with the slope down to the Menin Gate just visible on the right.

Colonel. The article soon came to the notice of the Battle Exploit Memorials Committee. This committee had been set up by the British government to select suitable sites for memorials, working in collaboration with the Imperial War Graves Commission.

However, nobody in either the Committee or the Commission knew anything about Beckles Willson or his plans. Irritated by this apparent intrusion into their sphere of responsibility, the Committee quickly issued instructions that the credentials of the Canadian should be checked. With almost equal speed, Canada's representative on the Battle Exploit Memorials Committee was soon able to confirm that Beckles Willson had no official mandate from his government at home and that he had more or less appointed himself as self-styled commandant of Ypres! The luckless officer was called to London on 15 October 1919 and was given a formal reprimand for his actions. Less than a month later he was demobilised from the army and returned to his native land, leaving behind him his pretty little bungalow on the Ramparts and his dreams of a Canadian national memorial at the Menin Gate.[23]

Towards a "zone of silence" and a monument at the Menin Gate

Nevertheless, for quite some time it seemed probable that Beckles Willson, Churchill, Dhuicque and their supporters would at least get part of what they wanted. Even when it became apparent that it would not be possible to purchase the ruined city in its entirety, the British remained determined to acquire the rights to certain key buildings. This situation was unlikely to change, as long as Churchill remained at the War Office. Not surprisingly, the ruins of Ypres stood high on the agenda of the Battle Exploit Memorials Committee. In July 1919 a delegation from the committee travelled to Belgium, to inspect the sites where the British wished to erect memorials. This inspection was to be carried out jointly with Colonel Demeur, the Director-General of the Department for the Devastated Zone. On 14 July 1919 an important meeting took place between the visitors from London and representatives of the Belgian government and the Ypres City Council. The meeting was held on the Market Square, in the heart of the ruined city. The British deputation was led by Sir. G. McDonogh, with Captain Lyon of the War Office as Secretary. Also in attendance were Major-General F.J. Duncan from the British Head-quarters in France, the Canadian W.B. Anderson, the New Zealander Westmacott, Sir Frederic Kenyon (Director of the British Museum), Fabian Ware (Director of the Imperial War Graves Commission) and Major Ingpen (the Imperial War Graves Commission representative in Belgium). On the Belgian side stood Colonel Demeur (Director-General of the Department for the Devastated Zone), High Royal Commissioner Eugène De Groote and Deputy High Commissioner Biebuyck, Colonel A. Slingeneyer of the Ministry of War, Senator Vinck (Belgian Association of Local Government Authorities), Town Clerk Versailles of the City of Ypres and the City Architect, Jules Coomans. Burgomaster Colaert was unable to attend, but he was in the city that day and twice received updated reports on the progress of the meeting.

Commissioner De Groote opened the discussions with a declaration to the effect that the Belgian government had decided in principal that both the Cloth Hall and St Martin's Cathedral should be preserved in their ruined state. In general, however, it was intended that Ypres should be rebuilt and even at this early stage there was a proposal that the new City Hall should be sited slightly to the east of the existing Cloth Hall. Given this intention to reconstruct, the key question was now this: how much of the city should be left in ruins to serve as a memorial and which parts of these ruins should be granted to the British government for their own commemorative monuments? After some discussion, it was agreed that the area between the Cloth Hall, the Cathedral, the Public Gardens and the Diksmuidestraat should be provisionally fenced off. Within this zone, an area would be allocated to the British authorities. Steps would be taken to ensure that no clearance or other reconstruction work took place within the zone, thereby preserving the ruins until a final decision over their future could be taken. Architect Coomans would provide the British with a plan, indicating the sector which had been designated for their use. The British government would provide posts and barbed wire for the fencing, but the actual work would be carried out by the City Council. Plans for a tram line through the Market Square were scrapped, since everyone agreed that this would damage the serenity of the ruins complex. The Battle Exploit Memorials Committee undertook to press the British government for a quick decision with regard to the use to which they intended to put their section of the ruins. All plans for prospective monuments would be forwarded to Brussels, whilst, in turn, the Belgian government would provide the British with a schedule of their own rebuilding programme for the fenced-off zone. At a later stage, British and Belgian architects would liaise more closely, to ensure that there was a degree of uniformity between the various different monuments. Where necessary, private property within the ruins complex would be compulsorily purchased, to allow the chosen monuments to be constructed. Finally, it was agreed that the Ramparts in their entirety would be temporarily left in their existing condition, until such times as the British government had decided which sections it wished to use, on the understanding that any proposals should be compatible with the local desire that the old town walls should be available for use as a walkway for the public.[24]

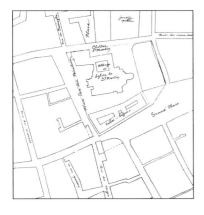

On *14 July 1919* the British and the Belgians agreed to fence off a section of the city centre, which would be left in ruins. City Architect Coomans marked off this "zone of silence" on his pre-war street plan.

Consequently, at this stage all options still seemed open. For the time being, the remains of the most important historical buildings and the Ramparts would be preserved in their war-damaged state, whilst the governments of both lands selected suitable locations and drew up suitable plans for the erection of monuments to commemorate their fallen. Moreover, it seemed highly probable that at least part of the city centre would be permanently maintained in ruins. To all intents and purposes, it looked as though Dhuicque and the "zone of silence" faction had won. However, one battle does not make a war and both camps realised that the campaign to decide the fate of Ypres would be long and hard. Nobody understood this better than Fabian Ware, the Director of the

The corner of the Meensestraat and the Kauwekijnstraat, *February 1919*. To the right stands the slope of the ramparts, where the Menin Gate would later be built.

Imperial War Graves Commission. Two days after the meeting in Ypres, he gave instructions to the Commission's local representative in Belgium that the pressure on the Belgian government should be kept up, by continually stressing the importance of the ruins issue to the British people. He further instructed that the minutes of the 14 July meeting should be jointly signed by all the participants and asked that every effort should be made to ensure that the promised fencing was erected as quickly as possible.[25] The Belgian side was equally quick to react. On 19 July Burgomaster Colaert wrote a strongly-worded letter of protest to the Royal High Commissioner, De Groote. According to Colaert, the compulsory purchase of private property within the ruin zone was out of the question. Furthermore, the city was only prepared to agree to the placing of a fence around this zone (and there only) as a purely temporary measure in the interests of public safety.[26]

The British had no intention of taking this kind of treatment lying down. Instead, they tried to force the pace. Less than a week after the Colaert letter, requisition forms were issued for the delivery of adequate quantities of posts and barbed wire to the city authorities in Ypres, so that the ruins could be properly cordoned off. In London, Architect Coomans' plan of the ruin zone was studied in great detail. According to the British – and contrary to the 14 July agreement – the Public Gardens did not appear to have been included within the designated area, but there was nonetheless general satisfaction that this former city park was already in the public domain (or so it was thought). Churchill was duly informed of the situation and gave instructions that this matter should now be brought to a swift conclusion. To enable a final decision to be taken, he asked that a memorandum should be prepared by the end of the following month (August 1919), in which the various possibilities offered by the different sites on the Ramparts and on the Market Square should be fully evaluated.

Asked for his opinion on this matter, Sir Frederic Kenyon, the Director of the British Museum, replied that not only would a British monument on

A sentry post guards the fenced-off "zone of silence" in the centre of the city, *1919.*

the Market Square be considerably more expensive, but that in all probability it would also have to compete with an equally imposing Belgian monument and with the new City Hall. In contrast, a monument on the Ramparts would be less costly and potentially more "exclusive". For a definitive assessment, he suggested that Reginald Blomfield, one of the leading British architects of the day, should be consulted.[27]

William Reid Dick, sculptor of the lion at the Menin Gate

Reginald Blomfield was one of the top architects of his day but is now largely forgotten. Much the same applies to William Reid Dick (Glasgow, 13 January 1879 - London, 1 October 1961), the sculptor of the lion which sits atop the Menin Gate in Ypres.

Very little is known about the personal history of Reid Dick. His work, however, is broad-ranging and widespread, although its generally conformist character does little to inspire curiosity about the man behind the artist.

That being said, it is indisputable that William Reid Dick was one of the leading British sculptors of his era – albeit as a representative of the overtly classical school. In what is probably the only existing monograph dedicated to Reid Dick, his work is described as "containing elements of Greek, Gothic and Renaissance sculpture, intertwined with original and contemporary accents".[79] The monograph (which dates from 1945) continued: "All in all, Reid Dick developed a style of his own, but it was a style that everyone could understand, although it still contained sufficient elements to satisfy those with more exacting tastes."
There is certainly ample evidence to show that his style at least satisfied the tastes of the British establishment, exacting or not. In 1939 he was appointed as the King's Sculptor in Ordinary for Scotland and later he received a knighthood.

Reid Dick's work – and the people who commissioned it – also make clear that he was a "darling of British high society". He was retained to carve the statues for the Kitchener Memorial Chapel in St Paul's Cathedral, including an elegant pieta in Portland stone and a figure of the legendary Field Marshal himself. He also made a bust of King George V for the Mansion House in London, as well as the effigy for the same king's tomb in St George's Chapel, Windsor. His busts of Winston Churchill and King George VI are equally well-known, although his favourite subject throughout his career was the "mother and child" theme.

Reid Dick was also responsible for a number of pieces of "public" sculpture, which still help to define the unique character of the streets of London. Some are animal scenes, like his famous composition for the Unilever Building near Blackfriars Bridge or his 1936 "Boy with Frog" fountain in Regent's Park. Other works are more "civic" in tone, such as his statues of Franklin Roosevelt in Grosvenor Square, of King George V at the House of Lords (1947) and of John Soane at the Bank of England. *The Herald* on the old Press Association and Reuter's Building in Fleet Street is also a Reid Dick original, as are the bronze statue of a mounted Lady Godiva in Coventry and a further statue of King George V in the Howard Davis Park in Jersey (1936).

The sculpting of the lion – from a full scale model – was actually carried out on top of the Menin Gate. A temporary work shelter was installed on the roof of the memorial, with extra large windows to provide plenty of light. (FOTO DANIEL, YPRES)

Nor was Reid Dick's work on the Menin Gate his only association with war memorials. He was also responsible for the war memorial at Bushey, which portrays the figure of a grieving woman. His Memorial to the Flying Services was a central feature in Lutyens' elegant memorial colonnade for the missing at Arras, depicting as it did a flight of doves soaring above the globe (a symbolic representation of the position of the sun on 11 November 1918). A similar Reid Dick design – this time a gilded eagle perched on a globe – was used for Reginald Blomfield's 1923 Royal Air Force Memorial on the banks of the River Thames in London.

Blomfield was greatly impressed with Reid Dick's work for the R.A.F. Memorial. The sculptor had succeeded in reproducing precisely what the architect had in mind.[80] It is hardly surprising, therefore, that Blomfield should again call on Reid Dick's services for the finishing touches to his great masterpiece at the Menin Gate. On 2 July 1924, Reid Dick reached agreement with Blomfield for the preparation of plaster casts for the lion and the sarcophagus at the Gate. The fee for the commission was set at £3,250 – a princely sum in those days.[81] This probably explains why only the lion would eventually be sculpted by Reid Dick himself. The sarcophagus and the other decorative elements were based on the Scotsman's models but were actually executed by a local Belgian workshop, Aumonier and Sons – altogether a cheaper option.

The final design for the lion underwent a number of modifications before actual carving. Whereas Blomfield's original 1921 drawings show the lion with its head resting sadly on its paws, Reid Dick's lion holds its head proudly erect. This was nonetheless still in keeping with Blomfield's request that the lion should not be "fierce and truculent, but patient and enduring, looking outward as a symbol of the latent strength and heroism of our race."[82]

The sculpting of the lion represents quite literally the crowning moment in the construction of the Menin Gate. It was only on 29 January 1927 – less than 6 months before the memorial's inauguration – that Reid Dick confirmed to the Imperial War Graves Commission that he would shortly be able to start work and that he would need approximately 12 weeks to complete his task.

The finished sculpture received praise from both the architect and the public: "the treatment of bold shadow-casting planes will be noticed, as well as its dignity of expression".[83] Nevertheless, the symbolism and significance of the lion has not always been universally understood and appreciated. Stefan Zweig, writing in the *Berliner Tageblatt* on 16 September 1928, commented that the lion looked as though it had dug its claws deep into its prey and was not planning to let go. This interpretation was a far cry from Blomfield's original idea that the lion should be seen as a "faithful guardian of British honour".[84]

Reginald Blomfield's proposals
for a monument in Ypres

By this point it was clear that the British – irrespective of whether a
section of the ruins were to be preserved – intended to erect a major war
memorial in Ypres. In the first instance, it was the explicit wish of the
Ministry of War that the eccentric genius of British architecture, Edwin
Lutyens, should be approached in connection with this task. However,
after much discussion within the Battle Exploit Memorials Committee, it
was finally decided that Reginald Blomfield, the Royal Architect, should
be asked to look at the Ypres project, with Lutyens' undoubted talents
being reserved for elsewhere. This was largely the doing of Fabian Ware.
Ware argued that Ypres, with its gothic associations, was more suited to
the classical, formal style of Blomfield than to the brilliant but sometimes
idiosyncratic designs of Lutyens. Furthermore, it was already planned that
Blomfield would visit Ypres in the near future, in order to inspect the site
of the cemetery on the Ramparts, for which he had been appointed "principal architect".[28] He could use this visit to kill two birds with one stone,
by examining the prospective memorial sites as well.[29]

On 18 August 1919 Blomfield confirmed that he would be happy to take
on the memorial project in Ypres. At this stage, the only idea he had was
that "the memorial should be something great."[30] During the first week of
September 1919, he made a four-day visit to the ruined town, during which
he inspected the following locations: the Market Square, the Lille Gate and
the adjacent British military cemetery, the island to the south-west of the
Lille Gate and the Menin Gate with its ramparts. He also talked at length
with City Architect Coomans and explained to him his initial thoughts
for possible monuments on the sites he had visited.

In his report to the Battle Exploit Memorials Committee, dated 25
September 1919, Blomfield advised against a monument on the Market
Square: "If the cathedral and Cloth Hall are rebuilt they would dominate
a memorial building in their immediate neighbourhood. If they are not
rebuilt, but are left as ruins, such an association would be unsuitable for a
memorial of the heroism of the British Army at Ypres."[31] Moreover,

because of the shape of the Market, the monument would have to stand opposite the Diksmuidestraat, "a narrow and insignificant street". By contrast, the Royal Architect was strongly impressed by the natural setting of the site at the Lille Gate, with its broad moat and its excellent view of the approaches to the city. However, there were a number of practical problems. The remains of the three circular medieval towers would hinder the construction of a memorial arch, such as Blomfield already had in mind. Furthermore, the walls of the Ramparts stopped at the eastern angle of the Lille Gate; to the west there was only a much lower and irregular earthen bank. Consequently, unless a new wall could be built, it would be impossible to devise a balanced design for the memorial. This aspect was further complicated by the presence of the nearby Ramparts Cemetery, since the positioning of this small burial ground substantially restricted the space available for the erection of any monument. According to Blomfield, the island opposite the Lion Tower (Leeuwentoren) also offered superficially attractive possibilities, but access was too difficult and it was too far from the centre of the city. He also rejected the idea that the whole Rampart area from the Lille Gate to the swimming baths should be incorporated into a grand memorial design, simply because it would be far too expensive.

Having eliminated the other sites, Blomfield finally came to the conclusion that attention should be focused on the Menin Gate and the ramparts in its immediate vicinity. The location was excellent: on a main avenue into the city, with a splendid excellent view from across the moat, but still relatively close to the centre. Moreover, the site was also heavily laden with symbolic significance: it was through this gate that hundreds of thousands of British soldiers had set off for the front, many never to return.

Having found the right spot, Blomfield proceeded to set out his plans for the memorial. What he envisaged was a gigantic "triumphal archway" (sic), erected on a causeway over the Citadel Moat (Kasteelgracht).[32] In this respect, it is worth noting that his original concept differed only slightly from the way the memorial would eventually be built – and can still be seen today. Originally, he foresaw four roof embrasures (in place of the existing three) and he made no mention of the stairwells in the northern and southern walls. Instead, he intended to use a series of exterior stair-

YPRES RAMPARTS

Blomfield considered the Lille Gate to be an excellent location for a memorial, although the lack of a rampart wall and the presence of both the Burgundian towers and the British military cemetery made the site impracticable. A view of Ramparts Cemetery, with the Lille Gate on the right.

cases on the city side of the memorial to lead the public up onto the ramparts. From here a further four stairways – one at each corner – would give access to the paved terrace of the monument, from where visitors could look out over the city and over the battlefields of the Salient. Partly as a result of the existence of the Canadian bungalow to the south of the Menin Gate (constructed by the redoubtable Beckles Willson), Blomfield also suggested that two additional buildings should be erected on each side of the central memorial, at a distance of about 230 metres. The northern pavilion would commemorate the exploits of the British divisions, whilst the southern pavilion – replacing the existing bungalow – would honour the Canadian forces. The ramparts between the pavilions and the central memorial would also be laid out in an appropriate manner. If this scheme proved too costly, or if the Canadians did not wish to give up their bungalow and its associated ground, then the plans would have to concentrate exclusively on the central structure, the giant archway. However, Blomfield stressed that he regarded this as a "last resort" solution – his very clear preference was for a scheme which incorporated the two flanking buildings on the ramparts. To back up this argument, he illustrated his report with plans and detailed drawings of various sections and elevations.

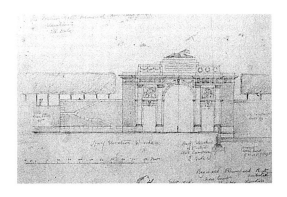

Blomfield's proposal for the Menin Gate, dated *September 1919*. (RIBA, London)

Several days later the Battle Exploit Memorials Committee confirmed its support of Blomfield's recommendations and the plans were forwarded to Churchill. The Secretary of State for War also looked favourably on the architect's work and decided to lay his proposals before the British Cabinet, together with plans for various other monuments in France and Flanders. And so it was, in November 1919, in the office of the Secretary to the Prime Minister in 10 Downing Street, that the members of His Britannic Majesty's Government were first able to cast their eyes over the plans for what would become the most famous of all British war memorials – the Menin Gate.[33]

By the end of 1919, Churchill had convinced his Cabinet colleagues that it was only right and proper that taxpayer's money should now be spent on the construction of the Menin Gate and on a whole series of other memorials, dedicated to the sacrifice of the British Army. To supervise this work, a new National Battlefield Memorials Committee was set up. This lead to a division of responsibility between the new committee, whose decisions were approved by the British government as a whole, and the existing Battle Exploit Memorials Committee, which was answerable solely to the Ministry of War. The task of this new committee – sometimes referred to as the Midleton Committee, after its Chairman, the Earl of Midleton – was to make recommendations to the government with regard to where memorials should be built, what form they should take and how much they would cost. There were a few prominent figures who had seats in both committees (the National Battlefield and the Battle

Exploit), but the new organ was perhaps most noteworthy for its absence of a representative from the Imperial War Graves Commission.

The British move away from their proposal for the preservation of the ruins of Ypres

At the end of November 1919, it was already apparent that the British were no longer concentrating exclusively on their original proposal to preserve the ruins of Ypres, but rather that they were moving towards the concept of a major architectural memorial at the Menin Gate. However, the Menin Gate project had been formulated under the auspices of the Battle Exploit Memorials Committee, which was only responsible to the British Ministry of War. Somewhat inconveniently, the planned memorial for Ypres now came under the jurisdiction of the new and more wide-ranging National Battlefield Memorials Committee. And although this committee was familiar with Blomfield's report and the follow-up action that had subsequently been taken, it was nonetheless deemed necessary to repeat the whole approval procedure, but this time at a higher, more public and more politically sensitive level. This promised to be no easy task.

By the autumn of 1919, British public opinion had become highly sensitive to all matters relating to war memorials. The Treaty of Versailles had now been signed, thereby "officially" bringing the war to an end. This was therefore the proper moment to consider how the fallen should be commemorated. The result was a veritable flood of newspaper articles, letters and meetings, many expressed in the most emotive terms. These public, almost cathartic outpourings – so well understood and exploited by the Beckles Willson's of the world – were also reflected in the political debate that followed. In the months leading up to Christmas 1919, there were no less than three separate parliamentary questions on this delicate subject (on 3 November, 12 November and 9 December).[34] If anything, this served to increase rather than to decrease public tension. And in this respect it is worth noting that the majority of British spokesmen and opinion makers were still in favour of retaining the ruins in Ypres. On 9 December 1919, 10 Downing Street even considered submitting a formal protest to the Belgian government, but ultimately instructed the Foreign Office to exercise more subtle diplomatic pressure.[35]

Hotel barracks and tourist buses outside the Menin Gate, *1919*.

However, not all Englishmen shared this "official" view. During a speech to commemorate the awarding of the Croix de Guerre to the City of Ypres, by the French President, Raymond Poincaré, Burgomaster Colaert related the story of an unnamed senior British officer, who is reported to have said: "I have always been strongly against the idea of preserving the ruins of Ypres, as a reminder to the world of the frightfulness of the Hun. The only reminder we need of the frightfulness of the Hun is a living specimen – that's the best example there is of the true German mentality."[36] As early as April 1918, another British officer, Captain James Lee, was also expressing his doubts about the ruins proposal. In his brief introduction to a historical note for British soldiers in Ypres, the then Town Major gave his opinion that the city should and would be rebuilt. "I greatly misunderstand the Flemish spirit, if it should not be."[37]

Nevertheless, for obvious political reasons, the British government was required to take account of the more widespread view in favour of preserving the Cloth Hall and the Cathedral in their existing condition. However, in this matter the hands of the British were effectively tied, since they could achieve nothing without the goodwill and co-operation of the Belgians.

And in Belgium at this time, the ruins of Ypres were just as much a source of fierce debate, as they were in Great Britain. There were numerous questions in the Belgian parliament on this thorny issue and the local papers were also full of emotive and emotional articles. In *L'Indépendance belge* on 12 October 1919, Eugène Dhuicque argued that any decision about the ruins of Ypres should be removed from the hands of the City Council: "These ruins belong to us all. Their fate should not be decided by just one city. The whole country must decide."[38] In contrast, a month earlier *Le XXe Siècle*, following an interview with Burgomaster Colaert, had published an editorial in favour of reconstruction. In Ypres itself, opinion was equally divided. An anonymous pamphlet in French and Dutch, printed in Bruges and signed by "a group of Ypres citizens", supported the idea of an extensive "zone of silence". It is perhaps worth noting that the terminology used in this pamphlet bears a strong resemblance to that of Beckles Willson, particularly with its contention that the ruins of Ypres were more historically important than those of Pompei.[39]

Whilst these public battles were being fought out, back in the corridors of power the Belgian and British authorities were also coming increasingly into conflict. Problems started almost immediately after the meeting in Ypres on 14 July 1919, when it had been agreed (or so it was thought) that the "zone of silence" should be fenced off. To ensure that this work was carried out, the British sought confirmation of the 14 July agreement at the highest national level. However, the Belgian government had no intention of being bound by promises made to the British at a local level. Consequently, the Ministry of Foreign Affairs replied that the Belgian negotiators in Ypres were not empowered to take executive decisions and that all agreements reached locally were subject to approval by Brussels.

In the circumstances, this approval was not likely to be granted quickly. Poor Major Ingpen, the War Graves Commission representative in Belgium, spent months and months in a valiant effort to persuade someone in authority to countersign the 14 July agreement. He never succeeded.

A second and related problem was the demarcation and fencing off of the agreed "zone of silence". Within days of receiving the plan from City Architect Coomans, the British had concluded that the Public Gardens – contrary to the agreement of 14 July – had not been included in the designated zone. This was not regarded as a major issue, since the "missing" area was already in the public domain (and had been since before the war). However, matters started to deteriorate when the British discovered that not even the remaining "incomplete" zone had been fenced off in full. In reality, only the Cloth Hall and St Martin's Cathedral had been cordoned off. The city authorities – who had carried out the work – informed the local British representatives that they had no power to place fences around private property and that the compulsory purchase of the property in question would simply be too expensive. Consequently, the British would have to be satisfied with a (temporary) prohibition of all rebuilding works. As far as other city-owned land to the north of the Cathedral and around the Public Gardens and the old Bishop's Palace was concerned, the city could see no reason why the local inhabitants should not have access to these areas. The British requested that at the very least a number of boards in three languages should be placed, reminding passers-by of the heroic deeds of the British Army.

The continued presence of these boards, together with the general condition of the ruins and the barbed wire fencing, were regularly checked by local officials of the Imperial War Graves Commission. If anything was found to be amiss, a report was promptly dispatched to London. The Department for the Devastated Zone and the City Council were also instantly informed. The Belgian authorities could have little doubt that the British were closely watching their every move.[401]

The crucial moment in this dispute – and also for the decision whether or not to preserve the ruins in a "zone of silence" – was likely to be the approval of the official building plan for central Ypres. Whether by accident or design, a plan which had already been approved in 1916 could no longer be found after the war. Consequently, a new plan had to be drawn up and approved – a task which would drag on until March 1921 (this was the single most important reason why the rebuilding of Ypres was so long delayed).

It was necessary that this new plan should be ratified by both the City Council and the Ministry of the Interior. The Council, supported by the Ypres Clubs[41], remained faithful to the original plan, as approved during the war years. This envisaged only minimal changes to the street layout and a faithful reconstruction of the pre-1914 situation. However, the Advisory Committee of the Ministry of the Interior, containing many of the most forward-looking Brussels architects, such as Eugène Dhuicque, favoured the inclusion a "zone of silence" in the new plan. Behind the scenes, the British also continued to exercise pressure on the Ministry in support of this latter option: as a result of the constant stream of letters which the Minister of the Interior personally received from the British Ambassador in the winter of 1919 and throughout 1920, he felt obliged to inform his ministerial colleague in Foreign Affairs "of the very great importance which the British government attaches to this matter." At a less exalted level, Major Ingpen of the Imperial War Graves Commission became an almost permanent (and not always welcome) visitor at the offices of the Department for the Devastated Region, as he attempted to discover the most up-to-date information about the ever-changing situation.

As a counterbalance to this diplomatic offensive by the British, the local population in Ypres (represented by the City Council and by the Ypres Clubs) increasingly began to make its voice heard. In March 1920 Minister Renkin promised a delegation lead by Burgomaster Colaert that the government would do all in its power to respect the wishes of the city's inhabitants, which effectively meant rejecting the idea for a "zone of silence". It seems likely that this promise by the Minister of the Interior had little to do with noble sentiment and everything to do with money. After the drain of the war years, the Belgian Treasury was almost empty: it simply could not afford the costly compulsory purchase measurs which the "zone of silence" would involve, especially as it quickly became clear that it would be months or years before reparation payments from the Germans could realistically be expected.[42]

Through various channels, the British government came to learn that the Belgian Ministry of the Interior was now only considering two options for the centre of Ypres:

1 The "zone of silence" idea, which would involve leaving the Cloth Hall and St Martin's Cathedral in ruins, set in a tree lined park, which would cover the area of the existing Market Square and the surrounding streets. This scheme would require the compulsory purchase of 65-70 properties, as well as an amendment to the official building plan. This was the proposal put forward by the advisors of the Ministry of the Interior.

2 The reconstruction of the city without amendment of the official building plan, which would involve the rebuilding of the houses on the Market Square, but not the Cloth Hall and the Cathedral, which would be left in ruins. This was the proposal put forward by the City Council. [43]

The British feared that if the second scheme was adopted, the ruins would quickly loose their artistic worth or that they would eventually have to be removed on grounds of safety. It was for this reason that the British Ambassador, on the instructions of Churchill, let it be known in government circles in Brussels that acceptance of the second proposal would cause unrest in public opinion throughout the British Empire.[44] In July 1920 the British Cabinet even considered sending a strongly worded letter of protest to the Belgian government, but eventually decided that it was not appropriate to treat a friendly nation in this manner. Even so, it was clear to the British who the real villain of the piece was – Burgomaster Colaert: "While it had been decided by the Belgian government to preserve the ruins of the Cloth Hall and the Cathedral as a memorial of the War, the Burgomaster of Ypres had succeeded in changing the decision in order to meet his proposal for rebuilding the town, including the houses fronting on the Cloth Hall and the Cathedral."[45]

Further evidence that the removal of the ruins would cause unrest in Great Britain came in the form of a parliamentary question submitted to the House of Commons by Evelyn Wood M.P. on 28 October 1920. Wood made clear that he was raising this matter because of the "considerable anxiety that exists in this country as to the permanent preservation of the remains of the Cloth Hall". In his reply, the British Prime Minister, David Lloyd George, confirmed that the Belgian authorities had temporarily agreed to retain the Cloth Hall, the Cathedral and the Ramparts in their existing state, pending a final decision by the British government with regard to the location of a British memorial in Ypres. Beyond this, he could say no more at this stage.[46]

In December 1920 there were further moves in high government circles in Great Britain to secure the retention of at least part of the ruins and to prevent the building of the Menin Gate. Sir Alfred Mond of the Office of Public Works, who had given the original Churchill scheme unconditional support back in 1919, now did all in his power to scupper the Menin Gate project and to revert to a ruin-based memorial. By this time the Cabinet had already agreed to allocate £300,000 for the building of national memorials, half of which would be spent on the Menin Gate. On 13 December 1920 a furious Mond wrote: "My department has in no way been consulted on this matter, nor has any kind of Parliamentary sanction been obtained and, inasmuch as the expenditure will fall on my Votes, I feel I must ask the Committee to reconsider the sum allotted, more especially in regard to the Ypres Memorial which seems to me far to exceed what would appear reasonable."[47]

Two days later, an even more influential voice joined the debate: King George V himself. In a letter dated 15 December 1920, he advised 10 Downing Street that he fully supported Sir Alfred Mond's disapproval of spending £150,000 on a memorial gate in Ypres. He also let it be known that in his opinion "the ruins of Ypres are in themselves a memorial to the gallant and successful defence of the Ypres Salient by the British Army." [48] Needless to say, the British Cabinet could hardly ignore the wishes of their own king!

Meanwhile, back in Belgium matters progressed slowly. In May 1920 the Burgomaster of Ypres had suggested to the British that the rebuilding of the Cloth Hall and/or City Hall at their expense might also be regarded as a suitable monument for their fallen countrymen. Perhaps not surprisingly, the British were not prepared to consider any such scheme.[49]

However, this unusual proposal had the effect of further delaying the approval of an official building plan for the City of Ypres. Still further postponements resulted from a variety of other factors: the resignation of Minister Renkin and his replacement by Minister Jaspar; the illness of Royal High Commissioner De Schoonen, who was formally responsible for the drawing up of the plan; the problems of compulsory purchase (in particular, who would pay what); the criticism of the progressive plans put forward for the St Peter's district of the city; and, last but not least, continued British pressure behind the scenes.

On several occasions during the course of 1920, the Minister of the Interior confirmed in writing to his colleague in Foreign Affairs that the eventual building plan for Ypres would have to take account of the wishes of the British. However, the signals emerging from the Department for the Devastated Zone were somewhat different. An internal memorandum of August 1920 argued that, since the British had given no indication that they were prepared to pay for the preservation of the ruins and the compulsory purchase of property that this involved, the Ministry should no longer feel itself bound by the British request. Instead, the Ministry should reply to all future approaches from London "in very general terms". The writing was on the wall: it was becoming clearer and clearer that the approval of the building plan for Ypres was likely to result in a total victory for the supporters of identical reconstruction.[50]

Even in England, events were moving in this same general direction. In February 1921 the National Battlefield Memorials Committee finally reached the same decision about Ypres as the Battle Exploit Memorials Committee, nearly 18 months before. There would be no British monument on the Market Square, but only at the Menin Gate. In their final report, the Committee justified this decision as follows: "This Committee had also considered the possibility of the Grande Place at Ypres as a site and some reconstruction of the Cathedral or the Cloth Hall, but the two latter alternatives have been abandoned, as they are less significant for the Army than the Menin Gate, and moreover the cost of rebuilding the Cloth Hall and the Cathedral should more appropriately be paid by those who destroyed them, viz., the Germans."[51]

On 15 April 1921 Ambassador Grahame informed the Minister of Foreign Affairs that the British Government now formally wished to withdraw its request to erect a monument on the Market Square in Ypres and that, consequently, the Belgian authorities need no longer feel obliged to honour their previous commitment to preserve the ruins in their existing state. [52] The matter was closed: the reconstructionists had won.

Nevertheless, it is worth noting that the Cloth Hall remained in ruins until the autumn of 1928. Moreover, further efforts still continued to be made to have the ruins maintained in perpetuity. In 1923 the matter was raised again in the Belgian parliament.[53] Even as late as 16 September 1928 – shortly before the start of rebuilding work on the Bell Tower – Stefan Zweig argued in a major article in the *Berliner Tageblatt* that the ruins should be left in place, as a testimony to the true horror of war.[54]

The lions
of the Menin Gate

34. YPRES. Anciennes Fortifications. Porte de Menin.

The Menin Gate circa 1900. The famous
lions sit each side of the roadway.

From 1862 (the year in which the old
medieval gate was dismantled) until
the outbreak of the First World War,
the Menin Gate was nothing more
than a 13-metre wide roadway driven
through the ramparts of the city. At
the foot of the embankment, where
the road crossed over the rampart
moat, stood two proud stone lions, each holding the coat of arms of the City of Ypres.
The lions were sculpted in 1822 by a Monsieur Dubois of Zennik and were originally
placed on either side of a monumental staircase on the Market Square, which until
1848 gave direct access to the first floor of the Cloth Hall and Bell Tower. This "architecturally impure" staircase was removed during corrective restoration work and in
1862 – after a number of years at an unknown location – the lions were erected on two-
metre high pedestals at the Menin Gate.

During the early months of the Great War, the lions must have become a familiar
sight to the British and French soldiers, who passed through the Menin Gate in their
thousands on their way to the front – and to their deaths. Legend has it that in
September 1914 a number of local citizens filled the mouths of the lions with bundles
of straw, in the belief that the Germans would never enter Ypres until the lions had
eaten all the straw.[86] Unfortunately, the Kaiser and his armies were no respecters of
folklore tradition: on 7 October 1914, with the bundles of straw still uneaten, a regiment of German cavalry swept through the Menin Gate and occupied the city – the
only day during the entire war that Ypres was in enemy hands.

The lions survived the First Battle of Ypres (October-November 1914) with little or no real damage. So much is clear from a photograph taken in February 1915 by Geoffrey Winthrop Young, commander of the Friends' Ambulance Unit. The photograph shows Young's friends, Rex Benson and Cornet Jackson of the 9th Lancers and Herbert Hertigan of the 4th Dragoon Guards, posing in front of one of the intact lions. Later in the war, Rex Benson would be involved in the arrest of the notorious German "spy", Mata Hari and after the Armistice would make a stir as a director of the Kleinwort Benson trading bank.

The Second Battle of Ypres (April-May 1915) also failed to knock the lions from their pedestals but by time of the Third Battle of Ypres (July-November 1917) the proud

British soldiers warming themselves at a fire, as a transport convoy passes through the Menin Gate. The lions have disappeared without trace. (IWM, LONDON).

guardians of the Gate had disappeared completely, lost in the mass of rubble to which the entire rampart area had been reduced.

For some time after the end of hostilities, the lions were left lying in the ruins of the Menin Gate. However, in 1920 they were recovered from the debris and were brought to the Cloth Hall, where they became a subject of some considerable curiosity. The northern lion had lost its right forepaw and its coat of arms, whilst the southern lion had been reduced to a head and a piece of its hind quarters. During the 1930's these remains were removed to the stonemason's yard of the De Plancke company, situated between the Cloth Hall and the Cathedral.

In 1936 the Australian diplomatic representative in Brussels, High Commissioner Bruce, asked the Burgomaster of Ypres, Jan Vanderghote, if the city would be prepared to donate the lions to the new Australian War Memorial in Canberra. The City Council agreed to this request and on 31 August 1936 the two lions, carefully packed into wooden crates, were loaded onto a train in Ypres station. In exchange for the lions and as a symbol of friendship between the peoples of Belgium and Australia, the City was presented with a 50 cm high statue of an Australian infantryman – universally known as "Digger". The figure was sculpted by C. Webb Gilbert and can still be seen in the In Flanders Fields Museum. The text at the foot of the base plate reads: "In recognition of a friendship that will never be forgotten, not even when the last "Digger" has died and the last grave has fallen in."

The Australian War Memorial was formally inaugurated on ANZAC Day in 1939, but the outbreak of the Second World War delayed its opening to the public until 11 November 1941. The northern lion from the Menin Gate stood alongside Will Longstaff's famous painting, *The Menin Gate at Midnight*. The more damaged southern lion was not placed on display.

The invalid souvenir-salesman, Henri Duprez, photographed with one of the old Menin Gate lions, now lying damaged near the ruins of the Cloth Hall, *3 september 1921*. (FOTO ANTONY D'YPRES)

The two Menin Gate lions, shortly before their departure to Australia. (FOTO GEORGES VAN RAES)

In 1985, it was decided that the lions of Ypres should be fully restored – an idea that had been periodically considered ever since their original shipment to Australia back in 1936. Two members of the Australian War Memorial staff travelled to Belgium to carry out the necessary background research[87] and in 1987 the commission was entrusted to the sculptor Lucas Zywuszko. The missing pieces were added in a manner which makes perfectly clear that they are a reconstruction. Moreover, these pieces have been designed so that they can be easily removed at a later date, should this ever be required. To preserve a degree of originality, the more minor war damage (caused by shell fragments, etc.) was not repaired. In December 1988, the restored lions were installed in pride of place at the main entrance to the War Memorial. Since 11 November 1997 they also stand guard over the Tomb of the Unknown Australian Soldier, who now rests in the central rotunda of the Memorial.

The two – now fully restored – lions at the Australian War Memorial. (AWM, Canberra)

The story of the Ypres lions came full circle on 10 and 11 November 1997, when the "new" Menin Gate met the "old "Menin Gate" in far off Canberra. On these days, three visiting buglers from Ypres played the Last Post at the Australian War Memorial. For the very first time the lions were able to participate in the ceremony that is played daily at the location where they once stood, so many years ago.

The building of the Menin Gate

In the spring of 1921 the British finally came to the same conclusion that they had already reached back in 1919. The plans for a "zone of silence" were definitively shelved and the future destiny of the Market Square and its ruins passed back into the hands of the Belgian authorities. From now on, the British would concentrate their attention exclusively on the construction of a great national memorial at the Menin Gate. Right from the very start, it was intended that the Gate should become Britain's most important war memorial. Ypres had already assumed a unique position in the British national psyche: the British had been in the city throughout the war, from beginning to end; every division in the British Army had served in the dreaded Salient, fighting four hard and costly battles. Ypres was for the British what Verdun was for the French: a symbol of national suffering (little wonder that it was to these two cities that King George V chose to award the British Military Cross). By 1918, more than 200,000 soldiers of the British Empire had lost their lives in the bloody fields beyond the Ramparts.

In contrast to the possible memorial sites on the Market Square, the Menin Gate location was wholly uncontroversial. As early as 1919 both the City Council and the Ministry of the Interior had confirmed their willingness to transfer the necessary ground to the British. This decision was made easier by a number of key factors. The land in question was already in public ownership, so there was no need for any costly compulsory purchase orders. Moreover, a monument at the old city gate would have no serious effect on the desire of the city fathers to rebuild the city in its pre-1914 image. In short, it was a solution that offered benefits to all the parties involved – a true win-win situation.[55]

All that still needed to be decided was the final shape of the memorial. The design of a city gate is inherently difficult. By their very nature, city gates often have to be enlarged or removed, to allow for the growth of the city or for an unforeseen increase in the flow of traffic. In Ypres the situation was complicated still further by the possibility that at some later stage the adjacent ramparts would be demolished or filled in, thereby robbing the monument of its architectural effect. Notwithstanding all these reservations, the National Battlefield Memorials Committee nonetheless came to the conclusion that a monument as a city gate offered the most interesting range of options. Consequently, when it was decided to hold a competition to find an architect for the memorial, the Committee specified that the design had to be in the form of a gateway or an arch.

Running parallel to these developments, a debate had started within the Imperial War Graves Commission about how the hundreds of thousands of "missing" soldiers – the soldiers with no known grave – could best be commemorated. In December 1918 it had already been suggested that the names of these soldiers should be engraved on stone tablets, to be placed in the military cemetery nearest to the place where they were believed to have died. Another, less feasible, suggestion was that a headstone should be erected for every soldier, irrespective of whether he had a known grave or not. A third option was a commemorative monument in each cemetery, a variant on Lutyens' Cenotaph in London, but engraved with the names of the fallen. For various practical reasons, none of these ideas were workable in practice. It soon became clear that the only viable way to effectively honour the missing was to centralise their commemoration on larger monuments in a limited number of specific locations, each monument dealing with a particular battle or a particular geographical area. So it was that the idea of the "Memorials to the Missing" was born. In January 1921 the Imperial War Graves Commission decreed that these memorials should take the form of "architectural monuments" in the shape of an arch or chapel, in which the names of the dead could be engraved on stone panels.[56]

It was both illogical and unnecessary that Ypres should be the site of two major British monuments: one a national memorial, erected under the auspices of the National Battlefield Memorials Committee, and the other a commemorative memorial to the missing, constructed by the Imperial War Graves Commission. It was sensibly suggested that these two separate projects should be merged and, after a brief deliberation, the relevant authorities agreed. The War Graves Commission was given overall responsibility for the construction of the Ypres monument, although the National Battlefield Memorials Committee retained a right of consultation and comment, which it exercised through a newly created Cabinet Advisory

Committee on the Memorials to the Missing. Only the representative from New Zealand failed to agree with this proposed new style of commemoration, preferring to adhere to the original concept that the missing should be commemorated in cemeteries near the place where they died. This explains why even to this day there are no New Zealand names on the Menin Gate. Initially, the Australian representative shared the same opinion as his New Zealand colleague, but he was eventually persuaded to fall in behind the majority.[57]

It was in the summer of 1921 that the Imperial War Graves Commission finally inherited the combined project for a national monument and a commemorative memorial at the Menin Gate. As one of the Commission's own Principal Architects, Reginald Blomfield, had submitted a proposal for a similar construction to the Battle Exploit Memorials Committee just two years earlier, it was decided that in the first instance these plans should be re-examined. An idea of the National Battlefield Memorials Committee that a competition should be held to appoint the architect was quickly dropped. Blomfield was asked to revise his 1919 plans and this he agreed to do. There was no longer any question of two subsidiary pavilions on the ramparts. All resources were focused on the monumental gate itself, all the more so since this structure now had to serve as the memorial to the missing of the entire Ypres Salient: a colossal and difficult task.

In May 1921 the Director of the Imperial War Graves Commission, Fabian Ware, had thought that the Menin Gate would only have to carry a little more than 10,000 names, the number of missing from the First Battle of Ypres (19 October - 22 November 1914).[58] Shortly thereafter, it was decided that the Gate would have to commemorate all the soldiers with no known grave, who fell in all four Battles of Ypres or who were lost during the intervening periods. As the Gate could only provide space for a maximum of 60,000 names, it was clear that this decision was not realistic. Plans were drawn up for a second memorial to the missing at Tyne Cot Cemetery (for those who died after 15 August 1917). When Tyne Cot also threatened to become too small, a third memorial was constructed at Ploegsteert, for the missing from the Ploegsteert-Armentières sector. The procedure to decide which soldier would be commemorated on which memorial was both long and cumbersome. As a first step, the official lists of those who died ("Officers died in the Great War" and "Soldiers died in the Great War") were compared with the index of graves held by the War Graves Commission. Soldiers who were listed as dead, but who did not appear in the Commission's records, were deemed to be missing. Thereafter, the war diaries of the various military units were consulted, to decide in which geographical area the soldier concerned had gone missing. The resulting details were then forwarded to the next of kin for verification. Only then would a list of soldiers per memorial be compiled, which in turn would be divided into soldiers per panel for the task of engraving. This was a truly monumental work, but by 1926 it had been completed.[59]

In January-February 1922 the final land tenure agreement for the Menin Gate was worked out between the British authorities and the Belgian government. Because the land in question currently belonged to the city of Ypres, it was initially deemed to be more appropriate in the context of the agreement that it should be acquired by the Belgian state. The state would then grant the Imperial War Graves Commission permission to build a monument on the site. It seems strange that this roundabout method of working should have been chosen: a direct agreement between the City and the Commission would have been much more straight-forward. However, the representative of the Commission in Belgium (no doubt remembering the difficulties that had recently been experienced in connection with the now defunct "zone of silence" and the approval of the official building plan) had warned some months before of "the obstinate exercise of power by the Bourgmestre, backed by the Town Engineer."[60] For this reason, he had suggested that all negotiations should be carried out with the national government and not with the city council. Later on, this attitude changed and the Commission was prepared to negotiate over the ownership of the site. As far as the British were concerned, they saw no problem with this ownership being transferred to the city, on the under-standing that they would retain a right of inspection. On 22 May 1922 the Imperial War Graves Commission finally obtained all the necessary permits at both national and local level – work on the Menin Gate could finally commence, although the land on which it stood was to remain property of the city. This final decision may have been influenced by a macabre discov-ery made during the preliminary ground survey. Three metres under the road Blomfield and his engineers stumbled across the bodies of 28 Belgian civilians. On 22 April 1915 – the opening day of the Second Battle of Ypres – they had taken shelter in "De Oude Wacht", a small cafe run from what had once been the old toll house at the foot of the ramparts. A direct hit flattened the building and buried all the occupants. A telling but poignant indication that the Menin Gate is undeniably Belgian soil.

In the meantime, Blomfield had begun to amend his original 1919 plans. In a new proposal, dated 2 November 1921, he no longer foresaw broad stairways leading from the city side of the monument to the ramparts, but instead planned to install four spiral staircases in the corners of the structure. These would not only allow visitors access to the ramparts, but also to the memorial terrace at a higher level. For the general appearance of his archway, Blomfield based his design on the 17th century Porte de la Citadelle in Nancy.[61] His revised drawings were studied by a sub-committee of the Cabinet Advisory Committee on the Memorials to the Missing. Initially, this sub-committee suggested that the single arch should be replaced by three arches. The architect considered this idea carefully, but finally decided that three arches would present too many difficulties. In particular, they would restrict the amount of light inside the central chamber, giving the impression of a tunnel rather than of a memorial hall. Moreover, the sheer bulk of the three arches would detract from the effect of elegant

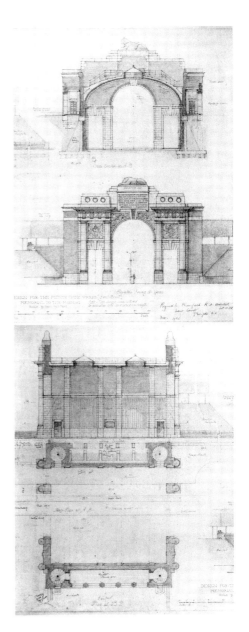

Design drawing for the Menin Gate by Reginald Blomfield, *1921*. There are several differences with the finished memorial: the number of roundels in the roof, spiral staircases, a recumbent lion, access to the roof,... (COLL. GUY GRUWEZ, YPRES)

61

majesty that Blomfield was trying to create. The cost would also be significantly higher. Persuaded by these cogent arguments, the sub-committee declared itself to be in agreement with the original scheme.[62]

On 20 March 1920 Blomfield set out his proposals in a meeting with the members of the City Council of Ypres and the City Architect, Jules Coomans. Coomans made a number of positive comments about the design, but nevertheless suggested that two major changes should be considered. Firstly, he asked that yellow bricks – typical for this part of Flanders – should be used instead of the red bricks envisaged by the Englishman. Secondly, he recommended that the stairways should be changed. For

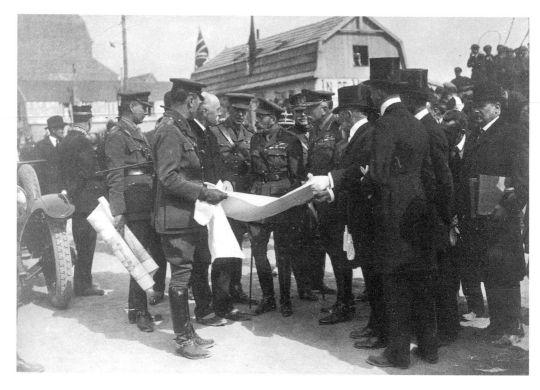

On *11 May 1922*, Sir Reginald Blomfield explained his plans for the Menin Gate to King George V, during His Majesty's visit to the Salient. Also visible in the photograph are Chief of Police Pierre Vandenbraambussche (extreme left, looking away), IWGC Director Fabian Ware (between Blomfield and the King), Field Marshal Sir Douglas Haig (right of the King), Burgomaster René Colaert (holding the plan) and City Architect Jules Coomans (right, bending over).

Blomfield, the first request was out of the question. However, he was far more open to the second suggestion. His initial idea for spiral staircases would be difficult to implement and to control. Moreover, these staircases would not give direct access onto the ramparts, which was not in keeping with the idea of the city that the use of the ramparts as a walking area should be encouraged. Consequently, Coomans proposed that the four corner staircases should be replaced by two broader stair-ways.

Coloured preliminary sketch of the Menin Gate, drawn by Blomfield in 1922 and presented to City Architect Jules Coomans – wrongly spelt as "Koomans" – in 1923.
(COLL. JEAN BULCKE, RENINGE)

These would climb away from both sides of the central hall, before splitting off to the left and right, leading directly to the ramparts, as the city desired. Notwithstanding the additional cost, Blomfield could appreciate the wisdom of this idea. Not only would the ramparts become more easily accessible, but the breech in the walls of the central hall would create an interesting architectural effect, without detracting from the overall integrity of the design. Above all, the new stairwells would provide more space for the engraving of names. Blomfield therefore agreed to the proposed change, thereby not only improving his memorial but also cementing his relations with an appreciative City Council.[63]

Nothing now stood in the way of the construction of the Menin Gate. On 28 July 1922 Blomfield signed a contract with the Imperial War Graves Commission for his work on the building, for which he would receive a fee equivalent to 5% of the total project costs (in return for which the design rights would become property of the Commission). The British company, D.G. Somerfield & Co., was engaged as principal contractor for the execution of the works, whilst a local masonry firm, De Plancke, was appointed sub-contractor. Dick Reid was chosen as Chief Sculptor.[64]

By early 1923 the planning phase had been completed and the laying of the foundations could begin. This was not without its difficulties. City Architect Coomans had assured his British colleague that the site of the memorial was bedded by a layer of solid clay. However, the earliest test drillings quickly revealed that the sub-strata were comprised almost entirely

The yard of the Ypres stonemasons company De Plancke during the construction of the Menin Gate. This company still exists and has premises just 200 yards beyond the memorial.

of running sand – the worst possible bedding for such a massive structure.[65] To solve the problem, Blomfield devised a raft foundation, held in place by four massive corner piles, each weighing more than 4 tons. By 1925 this giant raft was in position and building work could commence.

Meanwhile, a number of administrative matters still had to be finalised. In October 1923 the Nobel Prize winning writer, Rudyard Kipling, put forward his suggestions for the texts to be displayed on the memorial, in particular those for the eastern and western facades and for above the staircases in the central hall. Kipling had been involved with the Imperial War Graves Commission since its very earliest days and was deeply committed to its work, having lost his only son, Jack, with the Irish Guards at Loos. In due course, he was to write the texts for the majority of the Commission's memorials and headstones (a task which would be passed on to Edmund

Blunden after his death). As far as the Menin Gate was concerned, Kipling himself did not suggest the "Pro Rege, Pro Patria" texts for the east and west facades, but felt able to agree to their inclusion, when proposed to him by the Commission.[66]

Back in Ypres, the building work was by now well under way. The British undertook to maintain the roadway and the footpaths during construction and promised that traffic through the Gate would not be hindered. From this point onwards, no further design changes were made to the memorial, although in October 1924 a senior official of the War Graves Commission had suggested that a chapel should be added, for the use of visitors. At one stage, Blomfield did try to persuade Architect Coomans to alter the building line of the Meensestraat, since it had now become apparent that the Menin Gate would not be visible from the Cloth Hall and vice versa. To rectify this situation, the Englishman suggested that the building line along the northern side of the road leading to the Gate should be pulled back at its junction with the Market Square – just at the point, in fact, where Coomans was building the Court of Justice! The City Architect advised Blomfield in no uncertain terms that this was absolutely out of the question.[67] A further Blomfield proposal – that a plaza should be created on the eastern side of the memorial, just beyond the rampart moat – met with a similar fate.

Work on the Gate was also hampered by a number of other administrative and technical difficulties. There were delays in compiling the lists of the missing. Some of the stone for the name panels was of poor quality, so that they broke during the engraving process. In-painting of the inscriptions was held up by bad weather. An even more serious problem was the deval-

Rudyard Kipling confirms to Fabian Ware of the IWGC that he will write the inscriptions for the Menin Gate, 20 September 1923. (CWGC, Maidenhead)

The construction of the Menin Gate, viewed from city side. The traffic was not hindered. (FOTO DANIËL, YPRES)

A lateral view of the Menin Gate under construction. (FOTO DANIËL, YPRES)

The construction of the Menin Gate. Note the massive crane towering above the site. (FOTO DANIËL, YPRES)

Workers of the De Plancke firm pose proudly on the sarcophagus. (FOTO DANIËL, YPRES)

Work on the Gate, viewed from across the rampart moat. (Foto Daniël, Ypres)

Work in progress under the great central archway, viewed from the city side. Note the men on the extreme left: they are either engraving or colouring-in the name panels. (Foto Daniël, Ypres)

uation of the Belgian franc in 1926, which threatened to bankrupt the contractors paid in this currency. In January 1927 progress ground almost to a halt, as a result of a shortage of labour – most building workers preferred to cross the border into France, where they were substantially better paid.[68]

Whilst all this was going on, the British press had taken a close interest in the monument that was being built in Ypres. Public opinion was generally favourable, but there were exceptions. In January 1924 one correspondent wrote: "Look at the design! It is made up from the stock of architectural commonplaces and meaningless trappings, lacking that imaginative, sympathetic handling visible in all great works, bereft of the enthusiasm and patience which should endow it with the impress of life, lacking power and significance, missing utterly that quality which would prove it has been played over in every part by the sensibility of human intelligence and action."[69]

The criticism offered by the soldier and war poet, Siegfried Sassoon, in his poem *On passing the New Menin Gate* is altogether of a different order.

> *Who will remember, passing through this Gate,*
> *The unheroic Dead who fed the guns?*
> *Who shall absolve the foulness of their fate, –*
> *Those doomed, conscripted, unvictorious ones?*

> *Crudely renewed, the Salient holds its own.*
> *Paid are its dim defenders by this pomp;*
> *Paid, with a pile of peace-complacent stone,*
> *The armies who endured that sullen swamp.*

> *Here was the world's worst wound. And here with pride*
> *"Their name liveth for ever," the Gateway claims.*
> *Was ever an immolation so belied*
> *As these intolerably nameless names?*
> *Well might the Dead who struggled in the slime*
> *Rise and deride this sepulchre of crime.*

Although Sassoon was more or less a lone voice, it nonetheless made clear to the Imperial War Graves Commission that it was possible to interpret the memorial in a manner different to that which Commission itself had hoped and anticipated. It was for this reason that in May 1927 Major Ingpen, the Commission representative in Brussels, prepared a press release to explain the "true" significance of the Menin Gate. According to the good major, it was important that foreign journalists should avoid seeing the Gate as a kind of Arc de Triomphe, a celebration of military might and triumph. That would rightly be seen as an "offence to the next-of-kin of those whose names are inscribed upon it, and who, no doubt, consider it purely as a Memorial to their Dead, and in no sense a Monument of Victory"[70] – and this notwithstanding Blomfield's own stated intention that Gate should "symbolise the enduring power and indomitable tenacity of the British Empire."[71]

A frontal view of the almost completed memorial, shortly before the unveiling. (Foto Daniël, Ypres)

Perhaps the final word should be left to an outsider. In an article in the *Berliner Tageblatt* on 16 September 1928, the German pacifist author Stefan Zweig (1881-1942) wrote: "…Ypres has been bereft of her most renowned work of art. Henceforth no one will, as some did, make a pilgrimage to this out-of-the-way town only to see its magnificent Cloth Hall, standing there broad-shouldered, massive and mighty. In place of that which she has lost [= the Cloth Hall], however, Ypres has gained a new monument, and -let me say at once – one that is, both spiritually and artistically, profoundly impressive: The Menin Gate, erected by the English nation to its dead, a monument more moving than any other on European soil.

This gigantic gateway, lofty and of glistening marble [in fact Euville Stone], is erected over the road which formerly led towards the enemy. It overshadows the road – the road of invested Ypres, over which, alike in burning sun and rain, the English regiments advanced towards the front, over which guns, ambulance wagons and munitions were driven and numberless coffins were borne back. The broad vaulted gateway, Roman in the simplicity of its mass, towers on high, a mausoleum rather than a triumphal arch. On its front facing the enemy there lies on the summit a marble lion [in fact stone], his paw heavily planted as if on his prey which he does not mean to let go: on the reverse side facing the town stands a sarcophagus, gloomy and stern.

For this monument is to the dead, the six and fifty thousand English dead at Ypres whose graves could not be found, who lie somewhere crumbled together in a common grave, mutilated beyond recognition by shells, or disintegrating in the water, to all those who, unlike the others, have not their bright white polished stone in the cemeteries round about the town, the individual mark of their last resting-place. To all of these, the six and fifty thousand, this arch has been raised as a common tombstone and all these six and fifty thousand names are engraved in letters of gold – so many, so interminably many, that as on the columns of the Alhambra the writing becomes decorative. It is a memorial, then, offered not to victory, but to the dead – the victims – without any distinction, to the fallen Australians, English, Hindus and Mahommedans who are immortalized to the same degree, and in the same characters, in the same stone, by virtue of the same death. Here there is no image of the King, no mention of victories, no genuflections to generals of genius, no prattle about Archdukes and Princes: only the laconic, noble inscriptions – Pro Rege, Pro Patria. In its really Roman simplicity this monument to the six and fifty thousand is more impressive than any triumphal arch or monument to victory that I have ever seen, and its impressiveness is still further increased by the sight of the heaps of wreaths constantly being laid there by widows, children and friends. For a whole nation makes its pilgrimage every year to this common tomb of its unburied and unreturning soldiers."[72]

The Menin Gate 1927-...

24 July 1927:
the inauguration of the Menin Gate[88]

The inauguration of the Menin Gate on 24 July 1927 was undoubtedly a red-letter day for the citizens of Ypres. Thousands of British pilgrims arrived in the city and the B.B.C. erected a special transmission hut on the ramparts, so that the ceremony could be relayed live to Great Britain. In many British churches and other public places loudspeakers were set up, to allow people to follow events as they happened. Loudspeakers

The finished memorial awaits its unveiling. Wooden wracks stand ready to receive the expected mass of wreaths and flowers.

MENIN GATE MEMORIAL, YPRES.

OPENING CEREMONY
BY
FIELD MARSHAL LORD PLUMER, G.C.B., G.C.M.G., G.C.V.O., G.B.E.,
at 10.30 a.m. on Sunday, 24th July, 1927.

Admit_____to Enclosure No._____

This ticket admits one person only.
Ticket holders must be in their places by 9.30 a.m.

An entrance ticket to the unveiling ceremony.

IMPERIAL WAR GRAVES COMMISSION

ORDER OF CEREMONIAL
AT THE UNVEILING AND DEDICATION
OF THE MEMORIAL
AT THE

MENIN GATE, YPRES

BY FIELD-MARSHAL LORD PLUMER
G.C.B., G.C.M.G., G.C.V.O., G.B.E.

ON

SUNDAY, JULY 24th, 1927
AT 10.30 A.M.

THIS MEMORIAL IS ERECTED BY THE IMPERIAL
WAR GRAVES COMMISSION IN HONOUR OF
THE BRITISH ARMIES WHO STOOD AT YPRES
FROM 1914 TO 1918, AND OF 56,000 OF THOSE OF
THEIR DEAD WHO FELL IN THE SALIENT AND
WHO HAVE NO KNOWN GRAVE

The programme book for the unveiling ceremony.

were also set up in Ypres, as it seemed unlikely that the mass of expected visitors could all be accommodated at the Menin Gate. Deputy Burgomaster Sobry – Burgomaster Colaert was sick and would die on 3 September 1927 – encouraged local people by poster to deck their houses with British flags and to take an active part in the celebrations. The local weekly newspaper, *Het Ypersche/La Région D'Ypres* also suggested that "everyone should wear a buttonhole in the British national colours".

The Flemish Nationalist members of the City Council also used posters to announce that they, too, would participate in the ceremony and to encourage their supporters to do likewise. In a council meeting held a few days earlier, the goodwill of the Nationalists towards the British had been called into question by Deputy Burgomaster Sobry and the local Chamber of Commerce. The posters – printed in English – were designed to reassure British visitors that the Flemish Nationalists would indeed take part in the solemn commemoration of the Empire's dead, but as "anti-militarists".

This was not the only local dispute in the weeks leading up to the inauguration. At a council meeting held on 4 July 1927, the Nationalist and Socialist members had complained at the imperious tone used by the British authorities in their correspondence with the city. It was as though the British were treating Ypres as some kind of colony: in particular, their "commandeering" of the Town Hall for the opening ceremony without prior consultation with the city council was tantamount to an infringement of Belgian sovereignty. To make matters worse, it seemed likely that the inauguration would be turned into a thinly-veiled glorification of war – the question of honouring the dead hardly seemed to have been considered.

Deputy Burgomaster Sobry countered these criticisms of the Nationalists and Socialists, pointing out that the city should be grateful to be the recipient of such an impressive monument, a monument "which all the peoples of the world will wish to see and which will be more visited than the Lion of Waterloo, bringing goodwill and prosperity to our city for many years to come." Several days later the Chamber of Commerce put up posters in which they again openly accused the Flemish Nationalists and the Socialists of being anti-British, assuring the British – and particularly the Britons now living in Ypres – that the majority of the population did not share in these sentiments. The poster reminded its opponents of the events of 13 October 1914, when British troops had first marched into the city, to the loud cheers of the local people. An anonymous French article in *Het Ypersche/La Région D'Ypres* did much the same, going on to argue that tourism was one of the few sources of income available to the still ruined city: in these circumstances, it was madness to irritate the British.

The planning for the inauguration took months to complete. The St Barnabas Pilgrimage alone, in conjunction with the Ypres League, made arrangements for over 800 pilgrims to be brought to Ypres by special train and mail-boat. The honour of unveiling the memorial fell to Field Marshal Plumer. Originally, it had been thought that King George V might perform this task, but the King had decided as a matter of principle not to unveil any of his nation's war memorials and he did not wish to make an exception for the Menin Gate. How far this decision was influenced by his earlier opposition to the Gate and his desire to see Ypres kept in ruins remains an open question. Field Marshal Haig, the Commander-in-Chief of the British Army during the great and bloody battles of Ypres, was also overlooked, ostensible because he had inaugurated a memorial tablet in Brussels Cathedral only a few days before. King Albert I of Belgium was, however, amongst the guests of honour, as was Sir Laming Worthington-Evans, British Minister of War and Chairman of the Imperial War Graves Commission.

The royal party leaves the temporary town hall building to parade to the Menin Gate. On the first row (from left to right): the Governor of West Flanders, Sir Lamington Worthington-Evans, King Albert I, Field Marshal Plumer, Deputy Burgomaster Sobry.

Early on the morning of 24 July 1927, the workmen who had laboured so hard to build the memorial set about their final task: the placing of 4,000 chairs for the expected guests. It was clear in advance that this would not be enough: more than 15,000 pilgrims were anticipated. The relatively small BBC podium (with microphone) was positioned in the middle of the bridge. The inscription under the lion was covered with the flags of Great Britain, Belgium and France. To ensure that things ran smoothly, the organisers had issued four colour-coded cards, each of which gave invited guests access to a different part of the memorial enclosure.

Passing though the dense crowd of spectators, the parade arrives at the Menin Gate.

At 09.30 hours the guard of honour – made up of officers and men of a Belgian Carabinier regiment – took up position in front of the Town Hall (in the Kasselrij building on the Market Square, which now serves as a Commercial Court). Half an hour later, the guests of honour arrived and were formally welcomed, whilst other invitees took up their appointed places at the Menin Gate.

King Albert was introduced to the College of Aldermen, to Ambassador George Grahame of Great Britain, to Field Marshal Plumer, to Sir Laming Worthington-Evans and to the representatives of the British Chiefs of Staff and the Imperial War Graves Commission. The royal party then marched in procession to the Gate, via the Market Square and the Meensestraat (Menin Street), headed by the King, the Field Marshal, the British Minister of War, the Governor of West Flanders and the Deputy Burgomaster of Ypres. Behind them followed a whole train of civil and military dignitaries from Great Britain, Belgium and France, including

Sir Reginald Blomfield, designer of the memorial, and Fabian Ware, Director of the Imperial War Graves Commission.

On their way to the monument, the King and Field Marshal Plumer (who was staying at the legendary Skindles Hotel) stopped off to greet René Colaert, the Burgomaster of Ypres. By this stage, Colaert was already bed-ridden with the disease that would soon kill him, but he had insisted on being brought to a window, so that he could witness the unveiling of the Menin Gate, which he regarded as a crowning moment in his long fight to have his beloved city rebuilt.

At precisely 11 o'clock, the procession arrived under the shining white memorial. King Albert exchanged a few words with a number of British

The crowd awaits the arrival of the V.I.P.'s. Note how a part of the rampart moat near the Menin Gate stands dry, having been temporarily dammed during the construction phase. (CWGC, Maidenhead)

At the start of the ceremony, the congregation sings the hymn "O God, our help in ages past". The flags of Great Britain, France and Belgium cover the inscription under the lion. (CWGC, MAIDENHEAD)

war widows and the guard of honour took up its position on the south side of the bridge. The ceremony began with the hymn, "O God, our help in ages past", accompanied by the band of the 1st Battalion, the York and Lancaster Regiment. First to speak was the British Minister of War, who praised the architect and his design and who concluded by inviting Field Marshal Plumer to formally open the monument.

Plumer gave an emotional speech (learnt by heart), in which he spoke of the grief of

Field Marshal Plumer makes his speech, including the now legendary words: "He is not missing. He is here!". Sir Lamington Worthington-Evans and King Albert listen attentively. Behind Plumer and to his right (on the second row) sits Tubby Clayton, the founding father of Talbot House and the Toc H movement. (CWGC, MAIDENHEAD)

those who had no known grave to mourn, a grief which deserved the solidarity and respect of the entire nation. He expressed his opinion that the Menin Gate could help to lighten this burden of grief, an opinion encapsulated in the famous words: "He is not missing: he is here!" – a phrase that has ever since been closely associated with the memorial.

Field Marshall Plumer ended his address with the following sentences, which perhaps sowed the seeds for what later became the daily Last Post Ceremony: "No words can express our feelings adequately but they will be expressed for us by the familiar bugle calls which we shall hear on the conclusion of the service. The "Last Post" and the pipers lament are our tribute of mourning to our loved and honoured dead. The "Reveille" is a triumphant proclamation of our sure and certain hope of their resurrection to Eternal Life." With the press of a button, the Field Marshal allowed the flags to fall from the central inscription under the lion, revealing Kipling's simple but moving text: "To the armies of the British empire who stood here from 1914-1918 and to those of their dead who have no known grave." The Menin Gate was now officially open.

King Albert next read a brief word of thanks to the British nation (in English), and then the monument was dedicated and blessed by the Right Reverend J.M.Simms, who had been a chaplain to the British Army during the Great War.

King Albert reads his speech. English public opinion was favourably impressed by the fact that the King spoke in English. Fabian Ware – Director of the IWGC – can be seen in the left foreground. (CWGC, Maidenhead)

With the press of a button, Field Marshal Plumer unveils the dedicatory inscription – the memorial is now officially open.
(CWGC, Maidenhead)

A view of the crowds in front of the Menin Gate during the inauguration ceremony. (CWGC, MAIDENHEAD)

Field Marshal Haig, who was not present at the inauguration, had a wreath laid on his behalf. The inscription card was later removed and framed.

This was followed by the playing of the "Last Post", performed by the buglers of the 2nd Battalion, The Somerset Light Infantry and the centuries' old Scottish lament, "The Flowers of the Forest", performed by the pipers of the 1st Battalion, The Scots Guards. A heart-rending one minute's silence was finally broken by the strains of the "Reveille" and the singing of the Belgian and British national anthems.

The ceremony ended with the laying of wreaths and King Albert was introduced to those who had played an important role in the construction of the monument, including a number of the ordinary workers. Thereafter, the guests of honour were taken on a tour of the Gate by architect Blomfield. During the tour the Belgian monarch slipped a small box into Blomfield's hand, "rather in the manner that an indulgent uncle might reward a favourite nephew or niece for good school results." It later transpired that his box contained the Belgian Order of the Crown.[89]

The local press had only the highest praise for the day's events – there was hardly a word of criticism in any of the numerous articles which appeared. Later the same afternoon, at 15.00 hours, Field Marshal Plumer, in his capacity as Chairman of the Ypres League, laid the foundation stone of the new St George's Memorial Church and the Eton Memorial School.

On 28 July 1928 the City Council received a letter from Fabian Ware, the Director of the War Graves Commission, in which he expressed his thanks to the city and its inhabitants for the faultless organisation and smooth running of the inauguration ceremony. Deputy Burgomaster Sobry had the letter printed on a poster, which he then circulated throughout the city. Unfortunately, the Council had difficulty with the very un-Flemish name "Fabian" and so it appeared on the poster as a more locally understandable "Fabrice Ware".

Architect Reginald Blomfield leads King Albert I on a tour of the memorial. Fabian Ware of the IWGC stands in the background.
(CWGC, MAIDENHEAD)

The crowd under the Menin Gate, shortly after the end of the unveiling ceremony, *24 July 1927*.

Menin Gate at Midnight
(The Ghosts of the Menin Gate)
by Will Longstaff

Will Longstaff (Ballarat, 1879 - London, 1953) was an Australian painter of landscapes, allegorical works and war scenes.

During the First World War, he had served as a Captain in the Australian Imperial Force, where he occupied an important role as Camouflage Officer to the 2nd Australian Division.

He was also one of the few Australians present at the inauguration of the Menin Gate on 24 July 1927.

Menin Gate at Midnight by Will Longstaff.
(AWM, Canberra)

According to his own version of events, he was unable to sleep that night – such was the impression that the monument and the other war cemeteries in the region had made upon him. Around midnight, he got up and decided to go for a walk. His route took him back to the site of the new memorial. Whilst there he had a vision, in which he saw an army of dead soldiers rise up out of the ground in front of the Menin Gate and march off eastwards, back in the direction of the battlefields. Once he had returned to London, Longstaff decided to commit this vision to canvass. The result was *The Menin Gate at Midnight*[90], an allegorical painting based loosely on Field Marshall Plumer's famous remark during the inauguration of the memorial: "He is not missing, he is here!"[91]

The work enjoyed an instant and improbable success and has contributed in no small measure to the mythology surrounding the Menin Gate. Originally, the painting was only available for viewing in Longstaff's studio in Buckingham Palace Road, in London. It was also in London that the painting received its first widespread public exposure, when it appeared in the *Graphic Weekly* on Christmas Eve, 1927. Two weeks later, it was purchased by Lord Woolavington for the princely sum of 2,000 guineas – at that time, probably the largest amount ever paid for the work of an Australian painter.[92] The nobleman donated the canvass to the Government of Australia and for a time it hung in Australia House, home of the Australian diplomatic mission in London. It was here that the work was viewed with an approving eye by the members of the Imperial War Graves Commission – including architect, Reginald Blomfield – on 19 March 1928. A little earlier, King George V had asked for the painting to be brought to Buckingham Palace, so that he could view it in private. In April 1928 Longstaff's masterpiece was put on public exhibition in Manchester and in May it moved on to Glasgow, where it attracted more than 3,000 visitors per day during its two-week showing. On the eve of the tenth anniversary of the Armistice and scarcely a year after its creation, the painting appeared as a kind of mini-poster in the centrefold of the *Illustrated London News*.[93]

Success in England was followed by even greater success in Australia. During a three week period in February 1929, no fewer than 35,000 Australians queued up to view the painting in Melbourne Town Hall. Similar public exhibitions were later organised in Hobart, Launceston, Sydney and Brisbane. At the Sydney exhibition, the painting was displayed alongside a scale model of the Menin Gate, so that relatives could see the precise location of the panel on which their loved one was remembered.[94]

As a result of its popularity, hundreds of prints of *The Menin Gate at Midnight* were sold throughout Australia during the 1930's. The proceeds were donated towards the construction of the Australian War Memorial, the building where Longstaff's enigmatic work still hangs today.

1927-1940

The inauguration of the Menin Gate did not bring to an immediate end the problems that had surrounded its creation. The question of who would be the formal owner of the building – and who would therefore have the responsibility of guarding and maintaining it – still had to be officially decided. There were two obvious candidates: the War Graves Commission and the City of Ypres. The Commission had built the memorial, but it stood on ground that was owned by the city. Initially, the Commission was inclined to transfer all rights over the Gate to the Belgian State or to the authorities in Ypres. For this reason, in March 1926 the War Graves Commission placed the following text on the memorial, in both French and Dutch (the only Dutch text at that time to be found in the memorial precinct): "This Gate, erected by the peoples of the British Empire in honour of their dead, is donated to the citizens of Ypres to be an adornment of their city and a memorial of the days when the British Army defended it against the invader."[95]

However, in 1927 the City was not anxious to become the proud owner of this imposing structure – primarily because of the high cost of guarding it and maintaining it. After various discussions, a mutually-acceptable modus vivendi was reached: the city would remain the owner of the road running through the memorial, and would maintain it like any other piece of ground in public ownership; the memorial structure would remain the property of the Imperial War Graves Commission, which would therefore undertake its upkeep and maintenance.

Because no one had been specifically appointed to keep the area around the Menin Gate clean, by August-September 1927 a considerable rubbish problem had arisen. The road was covered with sand and old wreaths littered the footpaths and the stairwells. A first negative newspaper article on the subject appeared in *The News of the World*. According to their reporter, the Gate and its surroundings were filthy, whilst the visitors were constantly pestered by hawkers selling war souvenirs. On 20 September 1927, a second disparaging article (or rather a reader's letter) appeared in the *Times*, the newspaper of the establishment. *The News of the World* was one thing, but a letter in the *Times* could not be ignored. The Commission acted and acted quickly. A press release was drawn up and sent to all national press agencies. The release confirmed the broad outlines of the two articles, but pointed out that some remedial action had already been taken: on 12 September 1927 the City Council had passed a resolution forbidding the sale of war souvenirs within a 50 metre radius of the monument and also in the area between the Market Square and "The Bascule" (the bend in the road some 200 metres beyond the Menin Gate).

The Menin Gate on *21 September 1927*. (Foto Antony d'Ypres)

This, however, solved only part of the problem. In October 1927 Reginald Blomfield emphasised the need for a permanent and competent guard, "otherwise 'More Belgarum' the place will be treated as a latrine". Blomfield was also an advocate of the prompt removal of old wreaths, etc. and was strongly opposed to the placing of wreath stands in the central hallway and on the stairs.[96] The question of wreath stands would occupy Blomfield's thoughts for many years. As late as April 1939 he asked the Director of the IWGC, Fabian Ware (who frequented the same gentleman's club), to have these "horrible wooden stands" removed. The city had previously made a similar request, on the grounds that the stands were both unaesthetic and restricted access. In response, the Commission promised to investigate the possibility of fixing bronze hooks into the stonework of the main hall.[97]

September 1927 also saw another complaint, this time from a war-widow who claimed that the workmen engaged on the in-colouring of the memorial inscriptions wore "inappropriate" names painted on their overalls. To make matters worse, they sang raucous songs at the top of their voices. After a brief investigation, the Commission confirmed the validity of these comments, but argued that the singing wasn't very loud.

Right from the very beginning (and still today), one of the main problems was the noise of traffic passing through the Gate. Both the architect and the builders were aware of this problem, but both concluded (rightly, as it turned out) that little could be done. As soon as the work was finished and as soon as the first cars began to race under memorial archways, a heated public debate broke out. Matters were made worse by the fact that many cars tooted their horns as they approached the Gate, to warn the dozens of pilgrims standing on the roadway of their impending arrival. On 12 November 1928 Colonel L.H. Ducrôt summed up the feelings of many, when he described the resulting noise as "a desecration of the spirit of the place."[98] Clearly, it was impossible to make the Menin Gate a traffic-free area: the road through the memorial was the main – almost the only – access route into the city from the east. The presence of the ramparts also made alternative solutions difficult. The Commission's response was to suggest to the city authorities that the cobbled road should be replaced with tarmac, or that signs should be painted on the roadway, warning drivers to slow down.

Not that noise was the only problem caused by traffic at the Menin Gate. On 18 December 1934 a lorry drove into the memorial structure, causing substantial damage. The necessary repairs cost BF 450 – a not inconsiderable sum in those days.

The world-wide publicity given to the opening of the Menin Gate quickly led to a stream of visitors, all of whom wanted to see the famous memorial for themselves. Many of these were family and friends of the fallen, for whom the Menin Gate was the place where they could feel closest to the loved ones they had lost. Others were simply tourists and sightseers, anxious to see what all the fuss was about. As a result, the pious and the less pious descended on Ypres in droves. Some travelled individually; others – the majority – arrived as part of an organised "pilgrimage". The largest of these pilgrimages took place in August 1928. It was organised by the British Legion, which had been founded three years before as a central co-ordinating body for all veterans' activities. The pilgrimage – which lasted several days and visited various sites on the Western Front – culminated in a ceremony of remembrance under the Menin Gate on 8 August 1928: precisely 10 years after "the black day of the German army", when the tide of war finally turned in favour of the Allies. The 11,000 veterans and their

The British Legion pilgrimage, *8 August 1928*.

families all wore civilian dress: they did not want to give the impression that this was a victory parade, but simply wished to show to the world that their dead comrades had not been forgotten. The entire ceremony was broadcast live by the B.B.C. and was followed by a march-past in the Market Square, where the pilgrims were greeted by several high-ranking civil dignitaries: Crown Prince Edward of Great Britain, Prince Karel of Belgium and Admiral Sir John Jellicoe of Jutland fame, the new Chairman of the Royal British Legion.

Edward, Prince of Wales, and Karel, Duke of Flanders, during the march-past of the British Legion pilgrimage on *8 August 1928*.

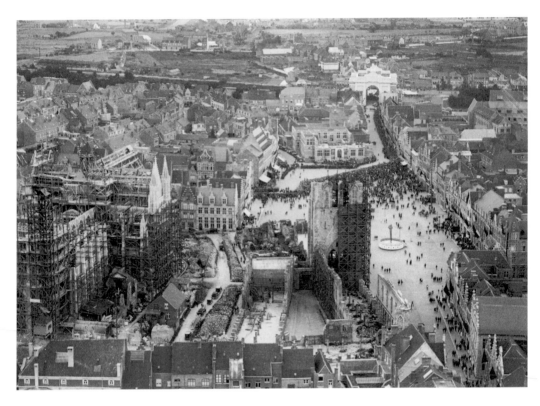

An aerial photograph of Ypres city centre, *8 August 1928.*

Burgomaster Sobry of Ypres described the whole occasion as "an example to the world of organisation, discipline, dignity and piety".[99]

During the 1920's the New Zealanders had decided not to commemorate their missing on the Menin Gate, but rather on a series of smaller memorials in cemeteries nearer to the spot where the soldiers had died. This decision rebounded on the New Zealand government once the popularity of the imposing new monument in Ypres became apparent. As a result, in January 1929 the New Zealand representative to the IWGC was required to request that consideration should be given to the placing of a bronze plaque under the Gate, so that visitors would know where the New Zealanders were actually commemorated.[100] A little later, a stone panel was inserted into one of the pillars in the main memorial hallway, bearing the famous fern-leaf of New Zealand and a short explanatory text.

If the Menin Gate was frequently in the news during its early years, more often than not it was mentioned in association with the Ypres League – an organisation which arranged many of the pilgrimages to the city and which was otherwise very active in the region. The Gate and the League became almost synonymous with each other, much to the chagrin of the members of the IWGC, who were actually responsible for the monument but who were scarcely ever mentioned. In July 1930, after yet another article in the *Times* concerning the fine work of the League in connection with the Menin Gate, the Commission seriously considered fixing a stone plaque to the wall of the memorial, engraved with the words: "This monument was erected by the Imperial War Graves Commission, on behalf of the peoples of the British Empire."

It will never be known with certainty how many people visited the Menin Gate during the years between its opening and the outbreak of the Second World War. However, some indication can be gained by an analysis of the visitors' books for the period. In July and August 1928, more than 23,000 pilgrims signed the book. For the year 1937, there were some 37,000 signatures in total.[101] And it must be remembered that not every visitor made an entry in the book – the true figure must be considerably higher. It is also interesting to note the strong seasonal variations in the totals: in August 1936 there were 18,832 visitors, whereas in December of the same year there were just 37, of whom only 3 were British. Hardly surprising, perhaps, in an era when overseas travel in general – certainly during the winter months – was far less common than it is today.[102]

It should also be remembered that not all the visitors to the memorial were British. German veterans also organised regular pilgrimages to the several German cemeteries in the region and almost invariably these groups made a point of paying their respects at the Menin Gate.[103] It is probably fair to say that such visits were not actively encouraged, but they were at least passively tolerated. Problems only began to occur after the rise to power of the Nazi Party in Germany, particularly during the period of growing international tension towards the end of the 1930's – a tension

A typical postcard of the Menin Gate,
as sold during the *1930's*.

caused primarily by the increasingly aggressive foreign policy of Hitler's Third Reich. Wreaths bearing the swastika emblem quickly disappeared from under the Menin Gate, much to the annoyance of the German authorities, who submitted an official complaint to the Belgian Ministry of Foreign Affairs in March 1939. On 8 April 1939, a group of German veterans laid a new wreath with a swastika ribbon, bearing the inscription: "Den tapferen Toten eines Ehrenwerten Gegners, Gewidmet von Deutschen Flandern Kampfern" (To the brave dead of a worthy adversary, from the German veterans of Flanders). The local police charged a certain Mr. Jeffries – probably the watchman appointed by the IWGC for the upkeep of the memorial – to remove the ribbon each night and to replace it each morning. Even so, within two days the ribbon was stolen. When the IWGC contacted the police and the public prosecutor, it was made perfectly clear to them that they had no authority whatsoever in matters relating to "desecrators and souvenir hunters". It was suggested that hooks should be fixed high on the memorial wall, to allow the wreaths to be placed out of reach of the public. However, before this could be done, the invasion of Poland in September 1939 promptly brought all further German visits to an end and so the problem effectively solved itself.

Some of the ceremonies at the Menin Gate during the inter-war period were a little curious, to say the least. In 1937 a group of Australian veterans asked to be allowed to burn a number of poppies, the ashes of which were then scattered at the Gate. On 10 April 1939, the French veterans association, "Les Defenseurs de Lille" (The Defenders of Lille) organised an equally strange event, during which a sack of earth from the battlefield at Verdun – brought to Ypres by bicycle – was buried in the lawn on the south side of the monument.

A ceremony at the Menin Gate before the Second World War.

By the mid-1930's – less than ten years after its inauguration – the memorial was already beginning to show signs of wear. In particular, the in-painting of the inscriptions in the stairwells was beginning to flake. This was understandable and to some degree inevitable, given that these open staircases – which led from the main memorial hall to the loggias – were fully exposed to the workings of wind and rain. Consequently, in reply to the many letters it received on this subject, the IWGC answered that the in-painting was primarily designed to improve the readability of inscriptions situated high up on the large name panels in the main hall. The panels in the stairwells were at a much lower level and could easily be read without in-painting. For this reason, it had been decided that these panels would no longer be repainted. Unfortunately for the Commission, the name panels were not the only things on the monument that were flaking. A report dated June 1939 makes clear that the plaster on the ceiling in the main hall was also beginning to peel.

At the Menin Gate

The year 1929 saw the publication of the play *At the Menin Gate* by S.N.Sedgewick: the twenty-second work in the series known as *Parish Plays*. *At the Menin Gate* was described as "a melodrama and a parable written for the League of Nations Union" and was intended for performance during a meeting of the said Union or at remembrance-related events. All the characters were intended to portray men and women from the "working-class".

The remarkable plot is played out in a small cafe somewhere near the Menin Gate in Ypres, a few days after the famous British Legion pilgrimage of 8 August 1928. A middle-aged British couple has travelled to Ypres with their daughter, Nelly, to remember their son, Bob, who was posted as "missing" in the Salient. The family is accompanied by William, who fought with Bob throughout the war and who is now trying to win the affections of Nelly. When Nelly rejects his advances, William attempts to blackmail her with a terrible secret: Bob's name is not recorded on the Menin Gate because he was a deserter. On the night of his death, he was supposed to be manning a vital observation post but he disappeared and his body was later found a few hundred yards towards the rear. If Nelly refuses to marry William, he will be forced to reveal the dreadful truth to her mother.

In the meantime, the family has become friendly with a Belgian waiter in one of the cafes near the Menin Gate. During the war, he had served as a translator with a British medical unit near the front. In the course of a meal in the cafe, the conversation turns to the attitude that should now be taken towards the Germans. The father hates them, but Nelly believes passionately in the noble cause of the League of Nations. Unexpectedly, a German couple enters the dining room, much to the annoyance and distaste of the father. The Germans ask for directions to the Menin Gate and leave.

In the face of Nelly's continued intransigence, William tells the mother the "truth" about her son, Bob: how he had run away from his post and how he would have deserved to be shot, were he not already dead. Whilst the family is coming to terms with this devastating news, the German couple re-enter the cafe, accompanied this time by their invalid son, Otto. The Germans explain that they come to Ypres each year, to lay a wreath in honour of an unknown British soldier, who had saved their son's life, as he lay bleeding to death in No Man's Land. The British soldier was himself killed, as he was carrying their son – his enemy – back to the safety of a medical post. Later on, in the field hospital, Otto had found the photograph of an unknown blond girl amongst his possessions. It must have come from the British soldier. At this point, the Belgian waiter intervenes. He was working as a stretcher-bearer that day – it was he who had pulled Otto out from under the body of the dead British soldier. When Otto finally shows around the photograph he has inherited from his noble British rescuer, the British family is amazed to recognise the portrait of a young Nelly! This unlikely tale ends with an Anglo-German-Belgian act of reconciliation under the Menin Gate.

1940-1944

On 23 July 1927, *Het Ypersche/La Région D'Ypres*, a local newspaper, had written: "The magnificent English monument at the Menin Gate is one of the best guarantees of Belgian independence... Will the powerful and noble British race ever allow that this memorial should be defiled by a foreign conqueror?" Even so, in May 1940 the British Expeditionary Force – unlike its predecessor 26 years earlier – would fail to halt the German Wehrmacht at the gates of Ypres.

British anti-tank guns at the Menin Gate,
May 1940.

As in 1914, Ypres played a not insignificant role in May 1940. On 21 May an important conference was held in the Town Hall, attended by most of the senior Allied commanders. At the suggestion of the French Commander-in-Chief, General Weygand, King Leopold III of Belgium (Commander-in-Chief of the Belgian Armed Forces), Lord Gort (Commander of the British Expeditionary Force) and General Billotte (Commander of the French forces in Belgium) came together to discuss new Allied tactics for halting the rapid and seemingly irresistible advance of the German panzers. The meeting ended inconclusively, without agreeing any clear or unified strategy. In the face of such indecision, the fate of Belgium – and of France – was effectively sealed. Two days later the first bombs fell on Ypres. The local population either sought shelter in the casements built into the ramparts or else fled the town. The British troops had occupied all key positions in the city and all the access roads and bridges had been wired with explosives. It seemed as if the British Expeditionary Force was again determined to defend the city at all costs.

At dawn on the morning of 28 May, the 6,000 local people sheltering in the ramparts were ordered by the British to evacuate the city. In view of the large number of sick people, old people and children, the First Alderman of the City, Gustave Delahaye, refused point-blank to accept the order. On the contrary, he encouraged his fellow citizens "to bear their breasts to the British bayonets and guns."[104] Perhaps it was thanks to Delahaye that the British abandoned their plans to hold Ypres to the last man, with all that would have entailed. The city still saw its fair share of fighting, but it was nowhere near as destructive as it might have been, without Delahaye's intervention.

Later that same day – 28 May – the Germans closed in on the outer suburbs and were resisted by men of the 50th Northumbrian Division, dug in along the ramparts. A battery of anti-tank guns covered the road that ran down to the Menin Gate, but it was all to no avail – the German pressure was simply too great. Under heavy shelling, Lieutenant David Smith led out a team of engineers to blow up the bridge in front of the memorial – an act for which Smith was later awarded the Military Cross. The Germans replied with machine gun and anti-tank fire from positions near the bend in the Menin Road and the Gate was hit several times (the damage was later repaired, although the work was carried out in such a manner as to ensure that these "scars of war" would remain permanently visible – as they still are).[105] During the night of 28/29 May, the British tanks withdrew from the city and on the morning of the twenty-ninth the swastika flew from the Bell Tower and from the spire of St Martin's Cathedral. Four years of occupation had begun.

The Menin Gate was damaged, but it had not been destroyed. The same could not be said for the bridge over the moat, which had been blown to smithereens – a pointless act, as the British themselves later admitted. For a time, the Imperial War Graves Commission – and the British people – remained unaware of the fate of their most famous and most well-loved war memorial. However, at long last, on 18 December 1940, the Director of the IWGC, Fabian Ware, received a report on its condition. The report had been drawn up on 3 September by the American chargé d'affaires in London (at that time, the Americans were still neutral and consequently were still able to travel to the Continent). The report advised that the memorial had indeed been damaged, but only slightly. On the Menin side, there were numerous pock-marks from shrapnel and three shells had hit the facade. The left cornice was also damaged, as was the lion (but only in one place). Various pieces of stone had also been shot off in the main memorial hall, but the name panels were fully intact. On the Ypres side, a shell had pierced one of the great stone columns and the northern support wall along the ramparts had been partially destroyed. The cenotaph was "shaken and broken", but the city authorities had carried out emergency repairs to prevent its further deterioration.

As soon as Ware received the report – which was accompanied by photographs – he contacted Reginald Blomfield. Blomfield commented: "I am glad it is no worse, and hope the Ypres people will not attempt to point it up with cement. The small holes, etc. could be left as scars of war, the larger ones should be dressed to rectangles and repaired with pieces of Euville stone cut to shape and neatly inlaid. It is good that the names are intact." It was Blomfield's last-ever pronouncement about the work which he himself regarded as his greatest masterpiece.[106]

The damaged Menin Gate, with its demolished bridge, *May-June 1940*.

The emergency repairs referred to in the report had been carried out in July and August 1940 by three stonemasons from the Ypres building firm J. Vandekerckhove and had been paid for by the City Council. In addition to replacing brickwork and cementing up damaged sections, the work had included " the removal of several swastikas." Clearly, not all the German soldiers had treated the monument with the respect it deserved.[107]

The 1940 repairs were only designed as temporary measures and the memorial was far from being restored to its pre-war condition. On 16 March 1942, the City Architect, Gabriel Gits, reported to the College of Aldermen that the spring thaw had caused several pieces of the damaged cornice to fall into the road. Moreover, further investigations had revealed that the cornice was covered with earth (deposited there following the blowing up of the bridge). This earth needed to be removed as a matter of urgency, not only to prevent further slippage but also to ensure that the water conduits remained free from obstruction. One such conduit had already plummeted to the roadway below and on the Ypres side another blocked pipe had resulted in water bursting through the pointing, so that the walls in the main memorial hall were becoming damp. Frost and water were also causing serious flaking to the roof of the hall. The College took note of Gits' report and in April and May 1942 further "stop-gap"

German troops repair the bridge over the rampart moat, *June 1940*. Note the damage to the memorial facade.

German troops leaving Ypres by the Menin Gate.

97

repairs were undertaken, including the sealing of the loggia doors with galvanised steel plate.[108]

After the war, a number of myths began to circulate in connection with the Menin Gate during the period of the German occupation. The first such myth was that the Germans, and not the British, had blown up the bridge over the rampart moat. As has been demonstrated above, this is patently untrue. Equally dubious is the story that someone fell to their death from the roof of the memorial. A third story – recently referred to in the British press – is that a German officer had one of his own soldiers shot for urinating under the Gate.[109] This, too, is without verifiable foundation. On the contrary, in general the Wehrmacht treated British cemeteries and memorials with respect[110], although the contention that German troops saluted every time they passed through the Menin Gate (as a number of people still claim) is perhaps taking matters a little too far.

One story that is true, however, is that during the war the Menin Gate was twice visited by no less a person than Adolf Hitler himself. The first visit took place on 1 June 1940, just a few days after the capture of Ypres and whilst the evacuation of the Allied armies from Dunkirk was still in progress. The Führer entered the city in an open car and drove via the Market Square to the Kauwekijnstraat. Alighting at the foot of the ramparts, he carried out a brief inspection of the damaged memorial, before proceeding with his retinue for a symbolically significant "pilgrimage" to the German military cemetery at Langemark (Hitler was also a Salient veteran, having fought at Wijtschate and Messines). A photograph of the Führer in the Kauwekijnstraat appeared on the cover of the Nazi Party magazine, *Der Illustrierter Beobachter* on 13 June 1940.

On 26 June the German leader was back in Ypres for another brief stopover. At around 16.30 hours he went for a stroll through the city with Hermann Goering, their route eventually bringing them to the Menin Gate. Goering himself would also return for a second visit – on 9 September 1940 – this time accompanied by the Japanese Ambassador. On this occasion, the Reichsmarschall hosted a banquet in honour of his Japanese guest at the Hotel Brittanique on the Market Square.[111]

Ypres certainly seems to have made a big impression on Hitler. On 4 August 1942, he is reported to have said: "I intend to send the architects charged with the rebuilding of Lübeck to Ypres. There they have more than 50 different colours for the roof tiles. Fifty! From salmon pink, right through to violet and gold. That new Ypres really is a fairy-tale city...."[112]

Adolf Hitler returns to his car in the Kauwekijnstraat, having just visited the Menin Gate, *1 June 1940.* (COLL. JO BOONE)

The Menin Gate: description and technical details

The Menin Gate is a large, rectangular gate structure, inspired by the triumphal arch-ways of classical antiquity. The monument has three central passageways – a road and two footpaths – and its exterior facades are faced with red brick and Portland stone. On the side of the memorial overlooking the Maarschalk Frenchlaan, the columns of the facade still bear the scars of damage caused during the Second World War. The central passageway – over the road – is surmounted by a semi-circular arch, finished with massive keystones. The two smaller, flanking passageways – over the footpaths – are surmounted by flat arches, also finished with massive keystones. The ordonnance of the facades is classical: massive Doric columns on high, square plinths, set under a roof construction with a heavily-profiled architrave and a frieze with triglyphs, interspersed with medallions and a continuous profiled cornice. On the underside of the cornice a lily (fleur de lys), a rose of union and other heraldic symbols are repeated in sequence. The crowns are comprised of alternate inset and protruding blocks of stone, the fronts of which are decorated with a laurel leaf motif. On the side of the memorial overlooking the Maarschalk Frenchlaan, the crown is surmounted by a recumbent lion, positioned so that it looks out over the old battlefields of the Ypres Salient. On the side of the memorial overlooking the Meensestraat, the crown is surmounted by a sarcophagus, mantled with a shroud and wreath.

Along each side of the structure, level with the rampart walls, a gallery (loggia) of six Doric columns in white stone has been constructed. The brick gable ends are provided with rectangular portals, finished with natural white stone copings. The portals, which give access to the gallery, are crowned with an open oak-leaf wreath, surmounted by trophies and a watchful lion. The columns are linked by a bronze railing, decorated with sitting lions. These lions are a replica of Alfred Steven's design for the balustrade of the Law Society Building in Chancery Lane, London. At each side, a double staircase links the main memorial hall with the gallery, ending with a spiral shaped balustrade in natural white stone. The steps are made from hard stone. Above each staircase hangs a cast-iron lantern.

The interior of the central memorial hall is faced throughout in natural white stone and is enclosed in a massive arched barrel vault, decorated with a coffer ceiling in reinforced concrete. The hall is lit by three large roundels, let into the ceiling. The edges of these roundels are lined with bronze.

On the eastern facade, two flower garlands hang above the roadway. Above the cornice there is a text panel, which reads: "To the armies of the British Empire, who stood here from 1914 to 1918 and to those of their dead who have no known grave." A pair of rectangular mirrors above the footpaths carry the texts: "Pro Patria" and "Pro Rege". Identical decorations and texts are also to be found on the western facade. Above the left-hand (northern) staircase in the central memorial hall, a further text reads: "Ad majorem Dei gloriam. Here are recorded the names of officers and men who fell in the Ypres Salient but to whom the fortunes of war denied the honoured burial given to their comrades in death." Above the opposite (southern) staircase, a complementary text panel is inscribed: They shall receive a crown of glory that fadeth not away." The western pillars (on the side of the Market Square) carry the following texts: "This memorial was built and is maintained by the Commonwealth War Graves Commission"; "Deze poort door de stammen van het Britsche Rijk ter eere van hun dooden opgericht wordt aan de burgers van Yper geschonken tot versiering van hunne stad en herinnering aan de dagen toen zij door het Britsche Leger tegen den inval beschermd werd" with dots between the words; "Erigé par les nations de l'Empire Britannique en l'honneur de leurs morts ce monument est offert aux citoyens d'Ypres pour l'ornement de leur cité et en commémoration des jours où l'Armée Britannique l'a défendue contre l'envahisseur" with dots between the words.

In the central memorial hall, in the stairwells and in the galleries, Portland stone panels, bearing the names of 55,000 soldiers killed before 15 August 1917, are set into the walls.[120]

Important dates and facts

June 1923: work starts on the foundations.
February 1924: work starts on the reinforced piling.
June 1925: the first layers of stone are positioned in the rampart moat.
October 1925: the first stone is laid in the central hall.
June 1927: finishing work is completed.
24 July 1927: unveiling.

The foundations of the Menin Gate are set to a depth of 12 metres (40 feet). More than 500 piles were driven into the ground, to provide added stability and support.

During construction, 500 tons of steel, 6,000 tons of stone and 11,000 tons of Portland cement were used. The total weight of the Menin Gate is 20,000 tons. Each of the support pillars for the main archway weighs 4 tons.

The height of the memorial, from the ground to the top of the lion's head, measures 25 metres (80 feet). The total width is approximately 31 metres (104 feet). The central Hall of Memory has a width of 20 metres (66 feet). The length of the memorial is 42.5 metres (135 feet, 6 inches). Each name panel in the main hall is 9.15 metres (30 feet) high.

The stairways from the central hall to the ramparts each contain 52 steps.

1944-...

On 6 September 1944, Ypres was liberated by troops of the First Polish Armoured Division, under the leadership of Brigadier-General Stanislaw Maczek – whose name in his native language coincidentally means "poppy". The general was well aware of the fate suffered by the city during the First World War and he gave his men clear instructions to cause as little structural damage as possible. These instructions were carried out to the letter – hardly a building was touched. This included the Menin Gate. In contrast to 1940, there was no serious fighting in the vicinity of the memorial – probably because the blown-up bridge had still not been properly repaired.[113]

The liberation of Ypres had been the subject of a "race" between the various Allied units. The Second Army had hoped that a British unit would be first into what they still regarded as a "British" city. The 53rd Welsh Division, setting out from Estaires, had made great efforts to beat the Poles, but only got as far as Wervik, Komen and Waasten. The 15th Scottish Division were even further wide of the mark. Believing that they were making for Ypres, they actually arrived at the River Lys at Halluin. Their divisional history records: "We were supposed to be crossing into Belgium by the Menin Gate, but the bridge over the River Lys had been blown and reconnaissance units were probing for another crossing-place."[114] Clearly, the unit had got its "Menin's" mixed up. Across the bridge at Halluin lay the town of Menin – the Menin Gate was some 20 kilometres further west!

As with Hitler, the city of Ypres made a huge impression on those British soldiers who were able to visit it. A soldier of the 14th/6th Queens Royal Regiment, arriving shortly after the liberation, wrote in his memoirs: "We stepped out onto a cobbled market square. The monumental gate through which we had driven lay some 300 yards behind us – an enormous arch of stone, glistening yellow in the sun. Suddenly, one of our party realised what the monument was – the Menin Gate. We were in Ypres. We stood on holy ground... On the Menin Gate we read the names of thousands of our men, who had died at the front near here. It made us feel very small..."[115]

On 11 September 1944, the *Daily Telegraph* was the first British newspaper to report that "the Germans have not defaced the memorial or the war cemeteries" in Ypres. Shortly thereafter, Fabian Ware, the Director of the IWGC, asked Austin Blomfield (son of Sir Reginald and his successor as Commission architect) if he would be prepared to travel to Flanders to inspect his father's monument and the other cemeteries in the area. Blomfield agreed, but was refused permission by the Ministry of Aircraft Production (for whom he was working at the time). It would be 1947-48 before Austin would finally get to have his say on the restoration work to be carried out at the Menin Gate.

It was only at the end of October 1944 that an inspection team from the IWGC was finally able to examine the memorial in detail. In addition to the damage previously reported, Works Maintenance Inspector Macfarlane also noted that the bronze doors to the loggia had disappeared and that the entrances were bricked up, although a hole had been knocked through in the north-west corner to give access to the stairs and the roof. The bronze railings and the register box had not been removed and were in reasonable condition. A number of name panels on the south side had been damaged by bullets and several pieces of stone under the lion (including the text) had also been hit or were hanging loose. The lawn and the hedges were all in an excellent state of maintenance. Macfarlane added that the damage had all resulted from the fighting in 1940 and confirmed that the bridge had been blown up by the British – an act, according to Macfarlane, that the local people regarded as unnecessary and futile. The explosion had also destroyed the walls on both sides of the bridge, but these had already been rebuilt at the initiative of Alderman Biebuyck. Biebuyck had worked as a partner of the British contractor, D.G. Somerville, during the original construction of the Menin Gate.[116] He had also made a significant contribution towards the fundraising for the new memorial, through the sale (with the architect's permission) of dozens of copies of one of Blomfields early design sketches.[117]

The repair works – regularly inspected by Austin Blomfield – began in June 1945 and continued until well into 1948. As a first step, 17 damaged name panels were replaced. Subsequently, the drainage was put back in order and the lion and the sarcophagus were carefully restored. In 1946 the double iron doors to the loggias were hastily reinstalled, "owing to the misuse to which the loggias are subjected by some people." All the stonework was carried out by a local firm, De Plancke and Sons. One of their masons was Maurice Baratto – a man whose life has been inextricably associated with the Menin Gate. He began working for De Plancke in 1927, when the original memorial was nearing completion. He was also involved in the repair works of 1945-48 (apart for a brief period in 1947, when he was employed by the Imperial War Graves Commission) and he was a bugler of the Last Post Association for more than thirty-six years (1944-1980).

A number of years ago Maurice let it be known that he and a number of his work-mates had bricked up a bottle in the masonry near the lion. The bottle contains a letter with the names of the 1948-work team and still sits in its lofty hiding-place – waiting to be discovered by some future team of restorers.[118]

A final important decision in respect of the Menin Gate was taken on 20 January 1949. On this date a meeting of the IWGC decided that no structural alterations should be carried out to the monument to reflect the events of the Second World War. The Menin Gate was a memorial to the Great War, and this it would remain. Only in the register was brief mention made of the damage sustained in May 1940.[119]

Since the 1940's, the Menin Gate has been regularly maintained by the staff of the now Commonwealth War Graves Commission: panels have been replaced, inscriptions have been repainted, the facades and the ceiling have been cleaned.

The progress of the restoration work is recorded for posterity by the IWGC. (CWGC, MAIDENHEAD)

In 1967 the Belgian postal service issued a stamp with a picture of the Menin Gate.

However, the general appearance of the memorial remains much the same as in 1927 and is unlikely now ever to change. Throughout the monuments long history, instances of vandalism have been few and far between. In 1975 the register – all 37 volumes – was thrown into the rampart moat, which led to the installation of better lighting in the main memorial hall. Even so, the register continues to be stolen, damaged or destroyed on a regular basis.

Perhaps the most famous incident occurred in 1983, at the height of the Cold War, when Belgium was gripped in a furious debate with regard to the siting of American cruise missiles. The words "Liever bomen dan bommen" (better trees than bombs) were daubed in large red letters across the stonework of the Gate. After an appeal in the local press, the culprits were quickly caught and (according to hearsay) heavily punished.

As an integral part of the ramparts (and not as a separate war memorial), the Menin Gate finally became a classified monument by a decision of 22 October 1986 (amended on 15 July 1987). This made good a promise that the Belgian Government and the Royal Commission for Monuments and Landscapes had originally made to Reginald Blomfield back in the 1920's, that the finished memorial would enjoy protected status. Better late than never.

The endless rows of nameless names

Some of the name panels on a postcard from the 1930's.

Perhaps the most poignant feature of the Menin Gate – the feature that makes the greatest impact on visitors and lingers longest in the memory – are the imposing name panels, with their almost 55,000 names. In this book, a conscious decision was taken not to give a precise figure for the number of soldiers commemorated on the Gate. This is simply not possible, given the frequency with which the figure changes. The Menin Gate is a truly "living" memorial. Occasionally names are added, if it becomes clear that a soldier has been overlooked, just as names are sometimes removed, if new and identifiable remains are discovered or if it can be shown that a soldier is incorrectly commemorated elsewhere. New names are added to the "addenda" panels, as soon as the omission has been investigated and confirmed. Names are only removed when the panel in question is replaced in the normal course of maintenance.

Mistakes on the Menin Gate

There have always been mistakes on the Menin Gate and there probably always will be. This is perhaps hardly surprising, in view of the huge numbers of missing soldiers with which the Imperial War Graves Commission had to deal. This is not to say that the

Commission was not careful during it compilation of lists for its memorials. On the contrary, the work was painstaking and thorough. The procedure for determining which name should be placed on which panel of which memorial involved no fewer than twenty-five well-defined, time-consuming and sometimes complicated steps.[121] In all cases the soldier's family and military unit were contacted and further lists were drawn up by region or organisation.

The decision to choose 15 August 1917 as the date for determining whether a soldier should be commemorated on the Menin Gate or on the Tyne Cot Memorial was finally taken in 1924, after a great deal of calculation and recalculation. Nevertheless, in 1925 it was discovered that the names of 800 soldiers from the London Regiment, whose names were included on the Menin Gate list, should actually have been commemorated at Tyne Cot. However, the discovery was made too late to alter the panel lists and so the Londoners remain on the Menin Gate – at least for the time being.[122] Sometimes the Commission was simply confronted by a lack of information. The panels on the Menin Gate for the 47th Sikh Regiment record just 15 names, although the regimental history states that on 26 April 1915 the 47th Sikhs lost no fewer than 348 of its 444 effective troops in heavy fighting north-east of Ypres. This discrepancy can only be accounted for by the administrative deficiencies that were not uncommon with units of the Indian Army.

Another frequent problem was the discovery that a soldier had a known grave after his name had already been engraved on a memorial to the missing. In many cases, it was several months or even years before a grave could be positively identified and for each cemetery there were extensive lists of graves that still needed to be found. There were also various instances of men being commemorated on more than one memorial.

On 29 September 1925 the IWGC was confronted for the first time with the case of a name that had been overlooked completely. W.C.Cannell had no known grave and his name was not included on the lists for the Menin Gate. Thanks to a letter from his sister, the error was discovered in time, but by February 1926 – still a year and a half before the inauguration of the memorial – the Commission had a list of no fewer than 120 names from 34 different regiments for engraving on the addenda panels.[123] This total would continue to increase and new names were regularly added.

Somewhat less common was the need to amend an incorrectly spelt name. One of the earliest instances related to a Canadian soldier, Private F. Schwardfager. His name was originally engraved as Swardfager, until the family wrote to point out the mistake.[124]

How to find a name on the Menin Gate?

If a visitor wishes to find a name on the Menin Gate, he first has to find this same name in one of the 37 memorial registers. These registers represent an alphabetical list of all the soldiers commemorated on the memorial. Registers 1-5 contain Canadian casualties, registers 6-9 the Australians, register 10 the South Africans and West Indians, register 11 the Indians and registers 12-36 the soldiers from the United Kingdom (including Ireland). Register 37 summarises the names that for various reasons could not be included in the other 36 registers before their publication. Once the visitor has found the name he is looking for, he will need to consult the introductory volume of the memorial register, to see on which panels the names for "his" soldiers regiment are listed. This introductory register also contains a plan which shows the location of these numbered panels on the memorial walls.

In total, there are 60 numbered panels. The smaller panels in the stairwells contain approximately 536 names, whilst the larger versions in the Hall of Memory and the loggias hold no fewer than 1,920 names. The letter type used for the engraving of the names was specially developed by the Imperial War Graves Commission.
Rather like with house numbers – and certainly with Belgian house numbers – the odd numbered panels are to be found on the left-hand side of the roadway (approaching from the direction of the Market Square), whilst the even numbered panels are all on the right-hand side. On the left, panels 1-15 and 15 A are to be found in the main hall, panels 17-33 in the stairwell and panels 35-59 in the loggias. The corresponding panels on the right are 2-16A in the main hall, 18-34 in the stairwell and 36-60 in the loggia. The four central pillars in the main hall were used for the commemoration of overseas troops (Indian, South African, West Indian), with the exception of the far more numerous casualties from Canada and Australia. The panels for these two dominion nations

are found alongside the panels of the British units, beginning in the central hall and continuing up the staircases. Soldiers from New Zealand are not commemorated on the Menin Gate, but are to be found on a series of smaller memorials in cemeteries nearer to the locations where they died. A panel in the main hall informs the public of this fact. These "diplomatic" arrangements were specially devised to ensure that troops from every nation of the then British Empire would be mentioned somewhere in the central Hall of Memory.

The units of the British Expeditionary Force are arranged in the order of precedence traditionally used in the British Army: first the cavalry, then the artillery, then the engineers, then the infantry and finally all other ancillary units. Cavalry and infantry regiments are further listed in order of seniority and thereafter by number. The Australian and Canadian infantry battalions are also listed by number, as are the battalions of the London Regiment. Per unit the names are listed alphabetically in order of rank. Soldiers with the same family name are ordered alphabetically, according to the initials of their first names. Soldiers who enlisted under false names are normally shown by the addition of the words "served as". The holders of the Victoria Cross are indicated by the additional letters "V.C." in front of the name, whilst other military decorations are indicated by their initial letters after the name. In each loggia there are two addenda panels (panels 57 and 59, and panels 58 and 60).[125]

The Menin Gate – open for interpretation

There are few monuments about which so much has been written and about which there are so many differing and contradictory opinions as the Menin Gate. This dualism is apparent in the very appearance of the memorial. First and foremost, the monument is designed to commemorate the dead. In this respect, its most important and impressive feature are the 60 name panels which record the details of those who were killed around Ypres and have no known grave. The sarcophagus which crowns the city-side of the monument also emphasises that this is intended as a place of mourning.

Even so – and notwithstanding the protestations of the Imperial War Graves Commission and others to the contrary – it is easy to see the Menin Gate as a monument of victory. Its aspect is undeniably that of a Roman triumphal arch. There is the watchful lion, looking out over the battlefields to the east, whilst the laurel wreaths and garlands of oak leaves are intended to symbolise courage and self-sacrifice. The inscriptions – "Pro Patria, Pro Rege" (For King and Country) – also lean in the direction of what the war poet – and war victim – Wilfred Owen called "the old lie: dulce et decorum est pro patria mori" (it is a sweet and seemly thing to die for one's country).

From its very earliest beginnings, the Imperial War Graves Commission has been anxious to avoid this interpretation being placed on its most well-known monument and has done all in its power to counteract the development of this school of thought.

Looking for the name of a loved one.
(Foto Daniël, Ypres)

According to the Commission, it would be an insult to the next-of-kin of the fallen if the memorial was to be seen as an Arc de Triomphe. The Gate was intended first and foremost as a place of commemoration for the many thousands of soldiers who had no known grave. Equally, it was a place where the relatives of the fallen could focus their grieving, a place where they could find comfort and solace. With the passage of time this function has become less important but it remains nonetheless relevant. Hardly a day goes by without one or more British visitors arriving at the Gate, to search for the name of their great-grandfather or great-uncle on the white stone panels. In this sense, perhaps the Menin Gate is not a truly military memorial. The names might well be arranged according to unit and rank, but in the first instance they are the names of family, and not of soldiers. After all, most of the men who died were not soldiers, but rather civilians in uniform, volunteers who had joined up only for the duration of the conflict.

In view of the dual nature of the memorial, it is perhaps not surprising that it has been the subject of a much varied comment and criticism throughout the years. On the day after its inauguration, Siegfried Sassoon referred to the new monument as "this sepulchre of crime", whilst in 1928 the German pacifist writer, Stefan Zweig, described it as being "profoundly impressive, both spiritually and artistically." Such contradictory points of view are a constant and recurring theme in the history of the Menin Gate.

The debate about the true nature and meaning of the Menin Gate acquired a new topicality during the 1980's, the decade in which the peace movement, inspired by a series of missile crises, reached its height. Why did protesters in 1983 choose the Gate to paint their slogan "trees, not bombs"? The implications seem clear. Similarly, when Pope John Paul II visited Ypres in 1985, he did so because of the city's self-proclaimed commitment to the cause of peace, a fact underlined during the Last Post Ceremony under the Menin Gate, when His Holiness prayed explicitly for world peace. In other words, it is clear that the Pope saw the memorial as a monument to peace, like many thousands of others who see those lists of "intolerably nameless names" as a powerful argument against the use of force in international affairs. Still others, such as the Ypres pamphleteer, Jan Claus, regard the Menin Gate as an expression of British militarism and imperialism, and are irritated and angered by the numerous parades and ceremonies which take place there.

Widely differing opinions about the Menin Gate will continue to exist, probably as long as the monument itself. The very least that can be said is that the Gate leaves no-one indifferent and that it provokes healthy and constructive debate on matters of contemporary relevance – all in all, no bad qualities for a war memorial.

The Last Post: a tradition for the future[126]

Today, the Last Post and the Menin Gate are inextricably linked with each other. Yet it was not always so. When the original plans for the Menin Gate were conceived, no consideration was given to the creation of a daily service of remembrance. The Last Post Ceremony grew up almost spontaneously from within the local community, a reverent reaction to the massive British memorial that had been placed in its midst.

The strength of the Last Post lies in the simplicity of the ceremony: the daily gathering of the buglers and the public in the same place at the same time; the stopping of the traffic; the high, clear notes of the bugles echoing around the imposing hall of memory with its endless rows of "nameless names", some 55,000 in all, each one a soldier of the then British Empire.
The effect created by this short but always moving tribute is impossible to describe in words – you really have to experience it for yourself. However, the history of the organisation which brought the ceremony into being can more easily be described – and it is a story well worth telling.

The first Last Post

The Last Post was played for the very first time under the Menin Gate during the inauguration of the memorial on 24 July 1927. The bugles made such an impression on the local chief of police, Commandant Pierre Vandenbraambussche, that he devised a plan whereby, together with a group of other local citizens, he would arrange for the regular playing of the Last Post at the memorial.

On 9 July 1927, the local weekly newspaper, *Het Ypersche/La Région D'Ypres*, had drawn attention to the only notice in the Dutch language (the language of Ypres) to be posted at the Menin Gate. The notice read: "This Gate, erected by the peoples of the British Empire in honour of their dead, is donated to the citizens of Ypres to be an adornment of their city and a memorial of the days when the British Army defended it against the invader." The paper was pleased that such an honour had befallen the city, but asked "how can we show our high regard and respect for the fallen, our gratitude to the great and noble British race?" Commandant Pierre Vandenbraambussche saw the answer in a daily ceremony.

He quickly gathered together a number of like-minded friends, sufficient to provide the necessary financial and logistical support for his new idea. Amongst them were Remi Boucquet, Aimé Gruwez (Chairman of the local Ypriana Brass Band), Richard Leclercq, (director of the local telephone and telegraph service), Hector Vermeulen (a local brewer and the driving force behind the Ypres Chamber of Commerce), Florimond Vandevoorde, Arthur Butaye (a lawyer), Armand Donck (another brewer), Henri Sobry (the Burgomaster of Ypres) and William Perrott (a captain in the British Army, who had stayed on in Ypres after the war).

Another early supporter of the initiative was Maurice Vergracht, commander of the local fire brigade. Vergracht placed the brigade's buglers at the disposal of Pierre Vandenbraambussche, and another local Englishman, Richard "Dick" Collick (an employee of the War Graves Commission) taught the firemen how to play the Last Post "in the English style" (Collick himself regularly played this salute to the fallen at remembrance ceremonies in Ypres during the 1920's).

Even today, there is still considerable confusion concerning the origin and status of the buglers, a confusion which dates back to the early days of the ceremony. The original buglers were most frequently referred to as "the buglers of the local fire brigade". Occasionally, they were alternatively described as "members of the Ypriana Brass Band". In fact, they were – and still are – buglers of the Last Post Committee. It is certainly true that all the buglers were members of the fire brigade but there were no formal links between the brigade and the Last Post Committee. It is equally true that the Ypriana Brass Band also lent a number of its buglers from the fire brigade and that these same buglers also played the Last Post under the Menin Gate. But again, there were no formal links between the band and the Last Post Committee. In short, the limited number of available local buglers at that time were effectively required to wear three different hats – one as members of the fire brigade, a second as members of Ypriana and a third as buglers under the Menin Gate. However, when the buglers played in this final capacity, they did so exclusively at the request of and on behalf of the Last Post Committee. When they stood under the Gate, they were not fire brigade buglers or Ypriana buglers – they were Last Post buglers. And so they still are today. During the years which followed the setting up of the ceremony, the informal ties with Ypriana gradually faded away but it is still a tradition that the Committee's buglers must all be members of the local volunteer fire brigade.

As soon as Pierre Vandenbraambussche and his friends had gathered together the necessary funds to pay the buglers and after the initiative had been introduced and favourably supported by the local press, the moment had arrived for the project to be launched.

At 20.30 hours on Monday, 2 July 1928 the first Last Post Ceremony was held.[127] On this opening evening there were approximately 70 spectators under the Menin Gate. Already in 1927, the Last Post had been played sporadically in Ypres and at the Gate, but only on important occasions. From now on, the ceremony would become a nightly event. During the very early days the buglers still played the Belgian version of the Last Post – Te Velde – simply because they were not sufficiently familiar with the British version. However, *Het Ypersche/La Région D'Ypres* newspaper reported on 7 July 1928 that the buglers had already switched to the British melody, although sadly it did not note the precise date on which this happened.[128]

The buglers took it in turns to play the nightly ceremony, dressed simply in their work clothes. This was intended to underline the fact that the Last Post was a spontaneous tribute from ordinary local people, not an official act of remembrance organised by some remote government body. Nevertheless, there were soon a number of requests – some from within Ypres itself – that the buglers should be issued with some kind of uniform, even if it was only an overcoat and cap to pull over their working dress.[129]

The high point of the first year was undoubtedly the great British Legion pilgrimage on 8 August 1928. Amongst those present was Crown Prince

Edward of Great Britain, later King Edward VIII. After the success of this occasion, it was decided to continue the daily Last Post ceremony until the end of September that year. There was just one exception. On 2 September, the buglers were required to perform at another engagement with the Ypriana Brass Band (of which they were also members) and so could not be under the Menin Gate at the appointed hour. Not surprisingly, this quickly produced a storm of reaction. A certain Colonel L.H. Ducrôt immediately wrote to the Imperial War Graves Commission, suggesting that British veterans should replace the local buglers: "If the ceremony is optional and fails to take precedence over other activities, the only answer is to make it an obligation."[130]

This was the first – but by no means the last – time that such British criticism would be levelled at the organisers of the Last Post Ceremony. There were regular complaints about the lack of a uniform and also about the fact that the buglers were locals, and not British veterans or employees of the IWGC.

However, all these comments failed to take account of the fundamental nature of the Last Post: namely, that it was a spontaneous local tribute organised by the people of Ypres. The Last Post melody might be British, the memorial where it was played might be British, but the Last Post Ceremony was very definitely Belgian.

Yet along with the criticism, there was also a good deal of positive reaction during the first year. In particular, many thousands of pilgrims were highly appreciative of the initiative and this persuaded the temporary organising committee that the ceremony should be restarted after its winter break.

This resumption took place on 1 May 1929 and since this date the Last Post has

M. M. les visiteurs sont invités à assister à la cérémonie du « **Last Post** » qui a lieu chaque soir sous le Mémorial de la Porte de Menin à 21 h. pendant l'été, à 20 h. pendant l'hiver.

Visitors are reminded that the « **Last Post** » is sounded every evening at the Menin Gate Memorial, at 9 o'clock during the summer and 8 o'clock during the winter months.
They are cordially invited to attend the ceremony.

De geachte bezoekers worden beleefd uitgenoodigd het « **Last Post** » te willen bijwonen, dat dagelijks plaats grijpt onder het denkmaal der Meenenpoort, te 8 u. 's avonds 's Winters, te 9 uur 's Zomers.

Drukkerij Dumortier, Yper

Announcement notice in three languages for the Last Post Ceremony, from the period before the Second World War.

A Last Post ceremony, carried out in all simplicity by their buglers in their every-day working dress. The Last Post was never an officially instigated event, but grew up as a spontaneous tribute from the people of Ypres to their liberators. On the left (in a straw hat) stands Pierre Vandenbraambussche, founder of the ceremony.

been played every evening under the Menin Gate, with the sole exception of the period of the German occupation between May 1940 and September 1944.

International recognition

Within a relatively short time, the impact made by the Last Post Ceremony was considerable and far-reaching. Newspapers throughout the British Empire published articles about "this unique event" and dignitaries from all over the world were keen to attend. Numerous special ceremonies were organised (mainly by veterans associations) to coincide with the daily playing and there were notices posted in every hotel in Ypres, informing visitors of the time of the ceremony and inviting them to take part. During the summer season, a travel operator in Blankenberge (on the Belgian coast) organised excursions to Ypres three times per week, with attendance at the Last Post being promoted as the climax of the visit. Little wonder, perhaps, that by the middle of 1929 six to seven hundred people were present at the ceremony each day.

Four buglers from the Grenadier Guards play the Last Post on the silver trumpets presented by the British Legion, *16 september 1929.*

A further view of the ceremony in which the British Ambassador handed over four silver trumpets on behalf of the British Legion, *16 September 1929.* On the extreme left stands Pierre Vandenbraambussche, founding father of the Last Post Committee.

On 16 September 1929 Lord Granville, the British Ambassador in Brussels, presented the Burgomaster of Ypres with four silver trumpets, which had been donated by the branches of the British Legion in Belgium. On this special occasion, the Last Post was played by the buglers of the Grenadier Guards, who thereafter presented the bugles to their Last Post colleagues. 39 years later, on 3 September 1967, one of the Grenadier buglers, Drum Major Tom Simpson, returned to Ypres and once again played his bugle under the Menin Gate.

The presentation of these four silver bugles lay at the basis of the decision to continue the ceremony through the winter months of 1929-30. To reflect this fact, the timing of the ceremony was slightly altered. Henceforth, from 15 May to 15 October, it would be held at 21.00 hours. During the rest of the year, it would take place at 20.00 hours. Moreover, each Tuesday and Thursday, volunteers from the local St George's Troop of the Boy Scouts would be present in uniform, to assist in the ceremony. At one stage, it was even suggested that these British scouts should be taught to play the Last Post, so that they could deputise for the buglers in case of emergencies.[131] Later that year, the ceremony would be attended by the British wartime prime minister, David Lloyd George and also by Lord Stamfordham, private secretary to Queen Victoria, Edward VII and George V.

One of the most important and difficult tasks for Vandenbraambussche and his friends was to raise sufficient funds to guarantee the future of the ceremony. To make this task easier, it was decided that the existing provisional administrative arrangements should be formalised. So it was that on 15 May 1930, in the temporary Town Hall in Ypres, the Last Post Committee officially came into being, under the high patronage of King Albert I of Belgium.[132] The Committee was set up as an independent, non-profit making body, and this it remains, even today. Founder Pierre Vandenbraambussche was elected as the first chairman, and the Board of Directors was made up by Richard Leclercq (vice-chairman and later chairman), Florimond Vandevoorde (secretary and treasurer, and also later chairman), Maurice Vergracht and Hector Vermeulen (chairman of the local Chamber of Commerce). The statutes of the new organisation were published in the Belgian Gazette on 30 May. The purpose of the Committee was stated as being "to maintain in perpetuity the daily playing of the Last Post Ceremony under the British memorial at the Menin Gate in Ypres, in honour of the soldiers of the British Army who died in Ypres or in the Ypres Salient during the war of 1914-1918." The Committee was divided into effective members, who had full voting rights, and associate members, who only had advisory powers. The Committee was required to have a minimum of five effective members, of whom at least 2/3 had to be Belgian.[133]

During the first formal meeting of the Committee on 26 June 1930, a full list of the associate and effective members was drawn up. Amongst the latter were Henri Sobry (Burgomaster of Ypres), Felix Vergracht (commander of the local fire brigade) and Aimé Gruwez (chairman of the Ypriana Brass Band and grandfather of the present chairman of the Last Post Association).
Two Britons were also included in the steering group: Lieutenant General Pulteney, a powerful figure in the influential Ypres League, and Major Paul Slessor, a leading light in the Talbot House movement (it was Slessor

who had managed to purchase the Talbot House building on behalf of Lord Wakefield in 1929).

On Remembrance Day 1930, the Last Post ceremony was broadcast live by Radio Belgique and by the B.B.C. For the first time, the Last Post melody was followed by the playing of the Reveille. During the first half of the 1930,'s, the Committee was tireless in its effort to get local people to attend the ceremony during the winter months and also to raise the necessary funds to keep the buglers paid. This was no sinecure, certainly during the hard years of the Great Depression. 1932 and 1933 were particularly difficult, and this notwithstanding a number of praiseworthy local initiatives (such as the proposal of a local British resident, L.N. Murphy, that on certain days half the proceeds from the newly opened war museum in Ypres should be donated to the Committee). However, there was also good news: in 1936 Pierre Vandenbraambussche was awarded the Order of the British Empire (an honour which was subsequently to be bestowed on all his successors as chairman). Vandenbraambussche also attended the 11 November ceremonies at the Cenotaph in London, a fact that was reported in almost every British newspaper.

From 1930 onwards, the daily ceremony was always attended by a member of the Last Post Committee, who was responsible for the necessary practical arrangements. Also on hand were a sergeant and two constables from the local police force, whose task was to stop the traffic. During the winter months, it was often the case that these were the only persons present under the Menin Gate. In spite of repeated appeals in the regional press, it had proved difficult to persuade the local populace to brave the cold winter weather. The members of the Committee even agreed that they should walk to the Gate each evening, in the hope that some of the local citizenry might feel inspired to follow their example. Particularly disappointing was the poor attendance of the large British community in Ypres. Fortunately, however, interest at official levels continued to grow: in 1930 the ceremony was attended by the prime ministers of Canada, Australia and New Zealand.

In the meantime, the Ypres Last Post Ceremony had become a subject for imitation elsewhere. On 12 November 1930, the *Times* ran an article in

A Last Post ceremony during the 1930's.

which it quoted a proposal by Fabian Ware, the Director of the Imperial War Graves Commission. Ware had informed the newspaper that there were plans for the daily playing of the Last Post at each of the Commission's 14 monuments to the missing in France and Belgium. As early as 1930, the Last Post had been played a number of times at the memorial near Loos, reportedly at the instigation of Rudyard Kipling, whose son was commemorated there. Shortly thereafter, the British Legion offered to provide the IWGC with two trumpets per memorial, on condition that the Commission would specially train members of its own staff to perform the daily ceremony. Subsequently, it was further suggested that a Scottish lament, played on the bagpipes, should also be added to the order of service. Fabian Ware quickly realised that this was a never-ending street. If a lament had to be played for the Scots, what about the Welsh and the Irish? Moreover, an official costing for the project in the autumn of 1931 revealed that the proposals were prohibitively expensive – and this for a series of ceremonies in remote and sparsely inhabited regions. Consequently, it was decided to radically scale down the scheme and a fund was eventually set up with the aim of financing the sporadic playing of the Last Post, but only at the larger memorials and only on special occasions. Yet even these more limited intentions ultimately came to nothing. By March 1934, only the Loos Last Post was still in existence as a daily ceremony, with occasional playings taking place at Villers-Bretonneux during special events. By the time the Second World War broke out, only the Last Post Ceremony in Ypres remained.[134]

In 1933, L.N. Murphy, Curator of the War Museum in Ypres, asked the Last Post Committee if it would be prepared to lend two bugles for an activity in London. The Committee refused point-blank. The Last Post was not an export product and would lose its special significance, if played away from Ypres. In contrast, proposals for the further promotion of the ceremony at a local level continued to flourish. Negotiations were opened with the provincial authorities for the introduction of a special "Last Post Train", which would transport visitors and tourists from Ostend to Ypres and back. Unfortunately, 1933 was a particularly bad year for tourism (thanks to the world economic crisis) and the proposals were quietly shelved.

Although the Committee's financial situation was far from poor, financial matters continued to dominate much of its thinking. A whole range of strategies were devised to raise additional funds. Right from the very beginning postcards had been sold to visiting pilgrims, but in 1933 a collection box was placed in Haig House (a main centre for British visitors to Ypres) and permission was requested for the placing of a similar box at Talbot House in Poperinghe. During the same year, a collection was also organised amongst the shopkeepers and hoteliers of the city, but the results were disappointing. In 1934 it was decided to publish and sell a photographic booklet of the ceremony, but this too achieved only moderate success.

Better news came from England, from where Major Paul Slessor informed the Committee that the Surrey Branches of the British Legion would make a donation of some £400 – a considerable sum in those days – during their pilgrimage to Ypres at Eastertide 1935. This generous donation helped to ensure that the Committee's investment fund finally showed a workable profit for the very first time. It seemed as though a corner had been turned. Further donations were received from local businessmen, from families of the fallen, from the City of Ypres and from various British Legion branches in Britain and Belgium. The levying of subscriptions from the Committee's local members also guaranteed that the fund would continue to grow on a regular basis.

However, these financial manoeuvrings were not without their repercussions. On 9 December 1934 an article appeared in the *Sunday Express* newspaper, which was highly critical of both the Last Post Committee and its daily ceremony. Under the headline "Belgium's tribute to the Ypres dead is bought with British money", the article condemned the proposed £400 donation by the Surrey Legion as scandalous, and went on to complain about both the shoddy clothing of the buglers and the fact that they were paid for their services.[135] At its meeting on 11 December 1934, the Committee decided to simply ignore the article.

The proposed hand-over of the Surrey donation went ahead as planned at Easter 1935 and was quite a major occasion. More than 400 British Legion members were present, as well as numerous civil and military dignitaries. The event was widely reported in the British press, as was a statement by the Last Post Committee that they no longer regarded the ceremony as being simply a tribute on behalf of the people of Ypres, but also on behalf of all British veterans who fought in the Great War. After the *Sunday Express* article, the Committee was pleased with this more positive publicity. It was less pleased, however, that city officials had pushed its members into the background at the Surrey ceremony. And it was totally unimpressed when the city tried to pass on to the Committee the costs of the subsequent civic banquet in the Town Hall!

These minor misunderstandings apart, 1935 was a good year for the Committee. On 17 October, the Belgian national radio station, NIR, broadcast an hour-long programme in French over the Last Post Ceremony, including a lengthy interview with Vice-Chairman Richard Leclercq.[136] Important visitors during the year included the Governor-General of New Zealand and the prime minister of Australia.

On 6 April 1936, Pierre Vandenbraambussche – the founder of the Last Post Committee and its first chairman – died after a short illness. He was succeeded as chairman by his deputy, Richard Leclercq, who was director of the regional office of the RTT – the Belgian telephone and telegraph service. Arthur Butaye was appointed as the new vice-chairman. Vandenbraambussche's death was reported extensively in the British newspapers, with obituaries in the *Times* and the *Daily Telegraph* – clearly, his work had been widely appreciated by the British establishment. Back in Ypres, the *Ypres Times* – the newspaper of the influential Ypres League – suggested that the IWGC should erect a plaque to Pierre Vandenbraambussche's memory at the Menin Gate.[137] Nothing came of this proposal, and consequently it was left to the headstone on his grave to make clear that this local chief of police should quite rightly be seen as the spiritual father of the daily Last Post Ceremony.

His place as an effective member of the Last Post Committee was filled by Burgomaster Jan Vanderghote.

†

TER ZALIGER GEDACHTENIS
van Mijnheer

PIERRE VANDENBRAAMBUSSCHE

Echtgenoot van Mevrouw ALICE HOSTYN

Politiecommissaris der Stad Yper
Officier van het Openbaar Ministerie
Voorzitter-Stichter van het « Last-Post Committee »

The obituary notice for Pierre Vandenbraambussche, Commandant of the Ypres Police and first Chairman of the Last Post Committee, *1936*.

On 20 May 1936 Duff Cooper, the British Minister of War, attended the Last Post-ceremony. A month later a complaint was received by the IWGC, concerning the unsatisfactory behaviour of some visitors during the playing of the Last Post. A brief investigation revealed that the problem lay with drinkers on the terraces of the nearby cafes. On 8 October 1936 the two British members of the Last Post Committee, General Pulteney and Major Slessor, were again required to write to the British press – this time in response to a letter in the *Times* – to explain why the buglers did not wear a uniform. In plain language, they tried to explain that the Last Post should in no way be seen as a "military" ceremony, where uniforms might be more appropriate, but rather as a simple tribute by two ordinary working men of Ypres, who had gone to the Menin Gate to bid the fallen "sleep well".[138] At about this time, the Committee also rejected a proposal that the ceremony should be held earlier, to make matters easier for the local hotel trade. The Committee members remained adamant that the Last Post must continue to mark the end of the day.

As the 1930's progressed, so the Last Post sought to broaden its horizons. The Committee put forward proposals that one of the bunkers under the ramparts should be developed into a museum, with a diorama of the Ypres Salient in 1918 and a reconstruction of a staff officer's quarters during the war years. Nothing came of these proposals, but the Committee did gradually become more and more involved with the tourist promotion of Ypres. Its chairman and secretary were co-opted into the newly created "Tourism Cell" and the ceremony began to be mentioned in local tourist literature (which, to the annoyance of the Committee, had not previously been the case).

In 1937, the Last Post Committee purchased BEF 100,000 of Belgian Government Bonds, the interest on which (when taken together with other donations) was sufficient to cover annual running costs.[139]

A year later, there were a number of musical difficulties. The British members of the Committee recommended that the buglers should undergo urgent retraining. The minutes of the Committee described the situation as follows: "Devoted as they are to their task, the performance of the Last Post has become something of a routine. Their playing contains little or

The Chairmen and Buglers of the Last Post Committee

Chairmen

Pierre Vandenbraambussche	1928-1936
Richard Leclercq	1936-1946
Jan Vanderghote	1946-1953
Florimond Vandevoorde	1953-1966
Guy Gruwez	1966-

Buglers

Eugène Angillis	1927-1940
Henri Lacante	1927-1940
Cyriel Demeulenaere	1927-1950
Joseph Arfeuille	1928-1955
Albert Catteeuw	1935-1960
Maurice Baratto	1944-1980
Daniel Demey	1945-1995
Antoine Verschoot	1956-
Jan Roose	1960-1968
Albert Verkouter	1966-
Martial Verschoot	1980-1987
Rik Vandekerckhove	1982-
Michel Ghesquiere	1983-
Dirk Vandekerckhove	1984-
Tony Desodt	1995-
Raf Decombel	2000-

no nuance. As a result, the sentimental phrasing, which characterises the Last Post, is lost. To put this matter right, and by virtue of the kind mediation of associate member Macfarlane, the buglers will receive lessons from Mr. Collick of the IWGC."

The results of the retraining are not recorded, but be that as it may, the Committee noted a falling off in attendance at the Last Post Ceremony towards the end of the decade.

1940-1944

On 4 April 1940, the Last Post Committee celebrated its tenth anniversary and held – for the time being – its final annual general meeting. A month later, German forces crossed the border and the Second World War in Belgium began. It was probably on 20 May – the day before the famous conference of Allied commanders in Ypres and a week before the fall of the city – that the daily ceremony was suspended. It would not be resumed for more than four years. Although the playing of the Last Post was not officially forbidden by the occupying power, and although the Germans generally treated British cemeteries and memorials with respect, it was understandable that the Committee should temporarily put an end to its activities: the ceremony could very easily have been interpreted as an open act of defiance or, at the very least, a gesture of support for the Allies. Nevertheless – and notwithstanding the enforced cessation in Ypres – that Last Post tradition continued to survive. Throughout the Second World War the Last Post was played regularly at the military plot in the cemetery at Brookwood, near Guildford, England (the Brookwood Last Post Committee still makes an annual visit to its sister organisation in Ypres, even today).

Ypres was liberated on 6 September 1944 by troops of the 1st Polish Armoured Division, under General Maczek. By early evening, the city had been cleared of German troops and the first British units were beginning to arrive. During the day, Mrs. Betsy Hahn, (a British subject who was married to a local hotelier, owner of Hotel "In de Maan" on the Market Square) had sought out Joseph "Fred" Arfeuille, one of the old Last Post buglers.[140] At her request, "Fred" played the Last Post under the Menin Gate at about 18.00 hours, whilst the retreating Germans were still less than 2 kilometres from the city. When the British soldiers heard the familiar strains of the bugle, they quickly went in search of "Fred" and, when they had found him, got him roaring drunk![141] Another version of events is that "Fred" had already "had a few" before he reached the Menin Gate. Carried away by the spirit (or spirits) of the moment, he went on to play the Last Post no less than six times, much to the delight of the assembled British, Polish and Canadian troops!

A column of Polish vehicles drives through the Market Square in the direction of the Menin Gate, to the cheers of the local people, *7 September 1944*.

Whichever version is true (and a summary of both was given in a newspaper article in the British *Daily Telegraph* under the heading "Memorials safe at Ypres"[142]) the Last Post Ceremony was officially resumed the following evening, in the presence of the British General Ross and the entire City Council, accompanied by large numbers of Allied troops and local citizens. This momentous occasion represents the final and definitive resumption of the Last Post tradition in Ypres. Since 6 September 1944 not a single day has gone by, without the Last Post being played under the Menin Gate.

During the first year after the liberation, attendance at the ceremony was high, as Allied troops flocked to Ypres (where many were also based). On 15 September 1944 the Last Post was played for a first time at midday, to mark the formal re-opening of St George's Memorial Church. It was also about this time that the Last Post was recorded by the B.B.C., so that it could be broadcast later from their studios in London.[143] It is also possible that Field Marshal Montgomery attended the ceremony, when he was briefly in Ypres at the end of 1944. The Remembrance Day celebrations on 11 November 1944 and the ceremony on 9 May 1945, the day after the surrender of Germany, were also memorable events during this immediate post-liberation period.

On 30 May 1945 the Last Post Committee held its first annual general meeting since the dark days of 1940. A number of the effective members had died in the interim, including the commandant of the fire brigade,

The first Remembrance Day ceremony after the liberation of Belgium: *11 November 1944.* (Coll. Maurice Baratto, Ypres)

The Last Post ceremony on *9 May 1945*, the day after the capitulation of Nazi Germany.
(COLL. MAURICE BARATTO, YPRES)

Felix Vergracht. To maintain its traditional links with the brigade, the Committee appointed the new commandant, Amedée De Plancke (a member of the same De Plancke family that had helped to build the Menin Gate) to the position left vacant by Vergracht's death. During the meeting, Chairman Richard Leclercq confirmed that no ceremonies had been held during the years of occupation, for fear of confiscation or even deportation by the German authorities.

The order of service for a Last Post Ceremony

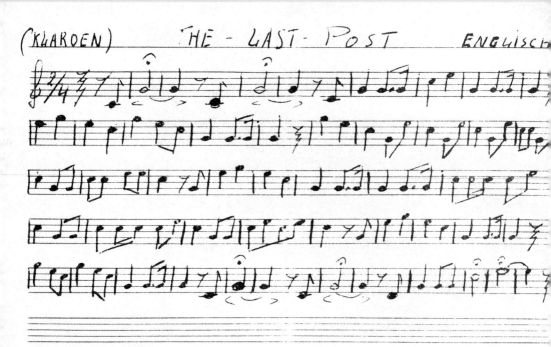

The public takes its place under the Menin Gate, but leaves the roadway and the entrances to the staircases free. The police stop the traffic at both sides of the monument. This is a symbolic moment, as the modern world pauses for a few seconds, to think of those who died. The buglers move to the centre of the road and take up position between the pillars on the moat side of the memorial, facing the city. The ceremony is ready to begin.

Although the buglers are all members of the city's volunteer fire brigade, and although they wear the uniform of the fire brigade on special ceremonial occasions, they do not stand under the Menin Gate as representatives of their service but rather as the representatives of the Last Post Committee – the association responsible for the organisation of the ceremony since its inception in 1928.

During the normal daily ceremony, only the Last Post is played.

During a "special" (i.e. more extended) Last Post Ceremony, a number of other elements can be added. The number and order of these elements can vary according to the circumstances.

The full order of service for a "special" Last Post Ceremony is as follows:

1 The buglers play the "Call to Attention".

2 If appropriate, prayers are said and speeches are given.

3 The buglers play the "Last Post".

4 As an act of remembrance, the exhortation is said, normally by a veteran (if present). The members of the public repeat the last line.

5 A minute's silence is held.

6 If a piper is present, the lament is played.

7 Flowers or wreaths are laid at the top of the stairs leading from the main memorial hall. During the wreath-laying, a hymn can be sung.

8 The buglers play the "Reveille".

9 The ceremony can be closed with the playing of national anthems.

The Last Post – which also forms the central element in the much simpler daily ceremony – was a bugle or trumpet call played in the British Army to mark the end of the day's labours and to call the troops back to their quarters. In military funerals and in the Last Post Ceremony it has come to represent a final farewell to the fallen.

The Belgian Army has its own equivalent of the Last Post – "Te Velde" – but even in Belgian military protocol the British Last Post still has a limited but specific role. As in Great Britain, it can be used during military funerals or it can also be played during an act of homage by a visiting foreign head of state at the Tomb of the Unknown Warrior in Brussels.

The Reveille was a bugle call played in the British Army at the beginning of the day, to rouse the troops from slumber and call them to their duties. In military funerals and in the Last Post Ceremony it has come to represent the return to daily life at the end of the act of homage. The Rouse is a shorter version of the Reveille.

The Exhortation is the fourth of seven verses from Laurence Binyon's poem *For the Fallen*. Robert Laurence Binyon (1869-1943) acquired fame as a poet and a dramatist, but was first and foremost an art historian, specialising in the painting of the Far East. It was in this latter capacity that he was employed by the British Museum. The poem *For the Fallen* was written as early as September 1914, but only became widely known after its publication in the *Times* newspaper on the first anniversary of the Armistice. It was viewed as a typical product of the "Lost Generation", the generation which was so cruelly disappointed by the outcome of the Great War, and it was subsequently set to music by Sir Edward Elgar. The fourth verse quickly became an established part of remembrance services during the 1920's and in 1928 the British Legion obtained formal permission from the author to both print and use this verse separately from the rest of the poem.[152]

For the Fallen

Laurence Binyon, September 1914

With proud thanksgiving, a mother for her children,
England mourns for her dead across the sea.
Flesh of her flesh they were, spirit of her spirit,
Fallen in the cause of the free.

Solemn the drums thrill: Death august and royal
Sings sorrow up into immortal spheres.
There is music in the midst of desolation
And a glory that shines upon our tears.

They went with songs to the battle, they were young,
Straight of limb, true of eye, steady and aglow.
They were staunch to the end against odds uncounted,
They fell with their faces to the foe.

They shall grow not old, as we that are left grow old:
Age shall not weary them, nor the years condemn.
At the going down of the sun and in the morning
We will remember them.

They mingle not with their laughing comrades again;
They sit no more at familiar tables of home;
They have no lot in our labour of the day-time;
They sleep beyond England's foam.

But where our desires are and our hopes profound,
Felt as a well-spring that is hidden from sight,
To the innermost heart of their own land they are known
As the stars are known to the Night;

As the stars that shall be bright when we are dust,
Moving in marches upon the heavenly plain,
As the stars that are starry in the time of our darkness,
To the end, to the end, they remain.

1945-1966

Notwithstanding the optimism and enthusiasm of the months following the liberation, it quickly became apparent that all was not well with the finances of the Last Post Committee. As a result of currency depreciation during the war, combined with the rising cost of paying the buglers, the Committee once again found itself faced with a deficit (albeit a limited one). To help alleviate the situation, Chairman Leclercq donated BEF 10,000 of government bonds to the Committee and a system of fee-paying subsidiary membership was introduced. Nevertheless, it would be a number of years before the Last Post finances were back in the black. Fortunately, the Committee could continue to rely on the generosity of its many benefactors. In 1947 one of its associate members, Colonel Barker, made a substantial donation of BEF 25,000. Several other members – including Major Brown, the Town Major of Ypres after the liberation – also dug deep into their own personal pockets.

Yet whilst the finances might gradually be recovering, attendance at the ceremony was moving resolutely in the opposite direction. By the end of 1946 almost all the Allied troops had left the country and few people had money over for "tourist" visits to Belgium during the immediate post-war period. In the meantime, the Committee had changed its official language of business from French to Dutch and had also appointed a new chairman. Richard Leclercq had died in the winter of 1946 and was succeeded in 1948 by Jan Vanderghote, Burgomaster of Ypres. During the brief interregnum, the meetings of the Committee were chaired by the most senior effective member, Arthur Butaye.

In the years leading up to 1950 very few special delegations attended the Last Post Ceremony. The number of tourists was also minimal. One bright spot was the presentation of two new silver bugles by the Blackpool and Fleetwood Old Contemptibles Association. The bugles in question had been purchased with a donation from a dock-worker, who had won a small fortune on the Littlewoods football pools (sad to relate, this old soldier later spent all his money on a series of wild schemes and died in abject poverty).

In 1953, Burgomaster Jan Vanderghote also died and was replaced as chairman by Florimond Vandevoorde, the last survivor of the original 1927 Committee.

A special Last Post ceremony in 1954. From left to right: Daniel Demey, Albert Catteeuw, Maurice Baratto and Joseph Arfeuille. (FOTO DANIËL, COLL. MAURICE BARATTO, YPRES)

In 1955 there were a number of difficulties with the buglers. One of them lost one of the 1929 silver trumpets, which had been entrusted to his personal care. As a result, half of his pay was stopped until he had paid half of the cost of a new instrument. The oldest bugler was also dismissed after repeated "incidents" under the Menin Gate.[144] On a more positive note, later the same year a new Last Post folder was printed – an encouraging sign of the growing revival in the tourist trade.

1956 was a year of high expenditure for the Last Post Committee. This was largely attributable to the manufacture of no less than 28,000 copies (in six different formats) of an engraving of the Last Post Ceremony by the Bruges artist, Albert Goethals (Goethals had been a liaison officer with the British Army in the Salient during the Great War and had agreed to donate any profits from the sale of his engraving to the Last Post Committee). Moreover, a number of the bugles – particularly those presented in 1929 – were in need of urgent repair. To make matters worse, another bugle went missing and needed to be replaced. Finances were clearly destined to remain one of the Committee's major headaches.

Happily, the second half of the 1950's saw a revival in the number of people attending the ceremony. This was also reflected in a growing number of V.I.P. visits. On 14 May 1957 the Duke of Gloucester, uncle of the British queen, was present under the Menin Gate and he was followed on 26 November by a delegation of British and Belgian parliamentarians.

In March 1959 a visiting pilgrimage of the Leeds Pals Association suggested that the Last Post should no longer be played under the Menin Gate, but rather on its roof or on the adjacent ramparts. This

The engraving of the Last Post by Albert Goethals, 1956.

would not only solve the problem of troublesome echoes but would also do away with the need to hinder passing traffic each evening. Chairman Vandevoorde politely rejected the suggestion out of hand. The stopping of the traffic was an important part of the symbolism of the ceremony, whilst the less accessible and less visible location on the ramparts would be inclined to keep a number of visitors away.[145]

Although the Last Post in Ypres was traditionally played on the bugle, on 11 November 1959 a certain Colonel W.M. Whitacker presented the Committee with two silver trumpets. The Colonel had served with the Royal Field Artillery during the Great War, and was keen to hear the Last Post performed on the trumpet, as was often the case in cavalry and artillery units. The buglers dutifully attended a number of practice sessions but were never really able to master the technique of the new instrument. More useful was the donation in spring 1961 of a further silver bugle by the Reverend Brenton, the then chaplain of St George's Memorial Church. Moreover, this bugle had a particular historic significance, having been used by the 15th Battalion of the Royal Welch Fusiliers during the Great War. Two further trumpets were received on 2 May 1961, presented on behalf of Colonel Edward H. Lancaster by Mr. Keiler MacKay, Vice-

Colonel W.M. Whitacker presents two silver trumpets to the Last Post Committee, *11 November 1959*. The Colonel poses in front of the temporary town hall on the Market Square with buglers and members of the Last Post Committee. From left to right: (first row) Valère Petit, Amedée De Plancke, Florimond Vandevoorde, Colonel Whitacker, Omer Robyn, Daniel Demey; (second row) Charles Vermeulen, Albert Catteeuw, Maurice Baratto, Trumpet Major Timmins, Archer Pothecary and Antoine Verschoot.
(COLL. MAURICE BARATTO, YPRES)

Governor of Ontario (Lancaster's home province in Canada). That same evening, the Last Post Ceremony was recorded by Belgian Newsreel Films.

In 1960 the Last Post Committee amended its statutes for the first time.[146] Henceforth, the Board of Directors would consist of ten members instead of the original five. The new directors were appointed just in time to take part in the celebrations to mark the 10,000th day of the Last Post Ceremony, which were held on 8 October 1960. As part of the festivities, a concert was given by the Regimental Band of the Somerset and Cornwall Light Infantry and their was also a modest exhibition, comprised of arte-facts from the personal collection of Dr. Alfred Caenepeel, a leading local historian and member of the Last Post Committee. Under the Menin Gate, the "anniversary" Last Post was played by no less than six buglers and two trumpeters.

In the spring of 1961, a certain Mr. Forster requested that the Last Post should be followed as a matter of course by the playing of the Reveille. This request was turned down.

As in all previous decades, the early part of the 1960's witnessed a search for new sources of revenue. Further income from new subsidiary members, from the City Council and from ever-generous benefactors eased the situation only marginally, and during the annual general meeting on 25 April 1963 Chairman Vandevoorde announced that the ceremony would have to be suspended, unless further funding was forthcoming. This alarming com-ment was picked up in the British media and letters appeared in several newspapers, principally the *Daily Telegraph*. Chairman Vandevoorde was quickly pressed into a retraction and on 13 July 1963 a letter from him was published under the heading "Menin Gate Ceremony will not end". In his letter Vandevoorde sketched a brief history of the Last Post but pointed out that costs were now seven times greater than before the Second World War. For this reason, the Committee had recently made an appeal to the people of Ypres for a special financial effort, particularly with an eye to the jubilee year of 1964, when numerous special Last Post Ceremonies were planned. This letter helped to allay some of the disquiet that had arisen in Great Britain, but not all. As late as October that year

Vandevoorde was still writing to the British Legion in London, to assure them that the future of the ceremony was safe.[147]

Nevertheless, all this commotion undoubtedly had the desired effect. An internal report of the Commonwealth War Graves Commission noted that it had passed on a substantially increased number of donations to the Last Post Committee in the months and years following the letters.[148] Fund-raising efforts in Ypres also met with greater success than previously, and, to cap it all, in 1967 the Belgian Postal Service agreed to issue a 1 frank stamp bearing an impression of the Menin Gate, the proceeds of which would be donated to the Last Post Committee.

In 1965 Florimond Vandevoorde announced that he wished to pass on the torch of responsibility to a younger generation. He remained in post until the election of a new chairman, Guy Gruwez, on 21 April 1966 and he officiated at a special Last Post a month later, which was attended by both the British and Belgian Royal Couples. The publicity linked to this high-profile media event was reflected in a further growing attendance at the daily ceremony (which had already been showing a significant upward trend since the beginning of the 1960's).

Representatives of the Canadian armed forces congratulate the Last Post buglers after a ceremony in 1963. (Coll. Maurice Baratto, Ypres)

The Last Post ceremony on *13 May 1966*, attended by both the British and Belgian Royal Couples.

1966-1985

The appointment of a new chairman saw a new wind sweep through the Last Post Committee. The buglers were issued with their own special badge and the order of service was revised, following consultation with the Commonwealth War Graves Commission.

From 1 September 1970, the time of the Last Post Ceremony was fixed at 20.00 hours all year round – a break with the 51-year tradition that the ceremony should take place at 21.00 hours during the summer months. During this same period, Maurice Baratto and Daniel Demey both celebrated their silver jubilee as buglers and to mark this event (at the invitation of Norwich British Legion) the Committee organised the first-ever Last Post "tour". In the course of 1969 this took the buglers and several of the Committee members to London, Norwich and Sittingbourne (Ypres twin city in Great Britain).

Earlier that year the Rotary Club in Sittingbourne had made a donation of £1,000 to the Committee's funds, which had resulted in a somewhat sensational headline in the *Daily Mail*: "Last Post at Ypres is saved by club's £1,000."[149] One of the few matters where there was no change during these years was in the question of uniform. Ordinary working dress remained the order of the day. However, it was agreed that for special occasions the buglers should wear their fire brigade uniforms.

On the publicity and public relations front, a new information board with details of forthcoming Last Post ceremonies in four different languages was erected near the Menin Gate in 1970. A number of visits were also made to local schools, in an effort to make the ceremony better known and better understood to a younger generation. Preparations for a new information leaflet were also put in hand.

The new chairman of the Last Post Committee, Guy Gruwez, in 1969. (COLL. MAURICE BARATTO, YPRES)

A rare event: the Last Post is disrupted by political protesters, *February 1972.*

At the beginning of 1972 an incident occurred at the end of one of the daily Last Post ceremonies. Members of a radical local youth club, together with members from the youth section of the Volksunie (the People's Front, a Flemish political party), wished to protest against the sending of British troops to Northern Ireland. At the end of the ceremony, they unfurled a banner with the text "Stop the murders in Ireland" and began to chant political slogans. This "desecration" was reported widely in both the British and Belgian press – thereby giving the protesters precisely the publicity they wanted – but was happily one of the very few instances where efforts have been made to exploit the Last Post for political purposes.

On 11 November 1973, the Remembrance Day ceremony from Ypres was broadcast live by B.B.C. Television. This resulted in a wave of positive reactions and placed the Last Post Ceremony firmly on the media map – from now on, television and radio performances would become a regular occurrence.

In 1974 the membership subscription was raised from BEF 100 to BEF 150 – the first ever increase since the subscription fee was introduced. Another innovation that year was the introduction of a kind of "summer uniform" for the buglers: a blue blazer. Because of the increasing number of special Last Post ceremonies and the number of ceremonies taking place at hours other than the standard 8 o'clock, the Committee felt obliged to introduce a number of measures to discourage such practices. At the same time, the dates and times of the special ceremonies that were agreed were now circulated on an official schedule to all interested parties, both inside and outside Ypres. Relations with the local authorities – and in particular with the Tourist Office – became somewhat strained during this period, mainly as a result of the late notification of visiting groups and the omission of the Last Post from much of the city's tourist literature.

Four of the Last Post buglers in 1974. From left to right: Maurice Baratto, Antoine Verschoot, Albert Verkouter and Daniel Demey.

On 13 June 1975 the Last Post was played for the 15,000th day. Because this anniversary coincided with the organisation of the legendary television game "Jeux Sans Frontières/It's A Knockout" in Ypres, the celebrations were fairly low-key. However, the anniversary did provide the stimulus for a new action in the local schools. Moreover, in a revised version of the multi-lingual information brochure, the Last Post Committee placed a new and broader interpretation on the meaning and significance of the ceremony. For the first time, it was specifically stated that the soldiers of the former enemy were also included in the act of homage. Furthermore, the hope was expressed that "by remembering the suffering that war has caused, the desire for peace will be strengthened in men and women of goodwill everywhere, so that the nations of the world may live side by side in mutual understanding and harmony".

During the second half of the 1970's, the Committee became aware of the growing need to train and recruit new buglers, to allow a gradual "changing of the guard", as the more senior buglers reached the end of their careers. This was long and patient work. Not only was it difficult to find younger people who were sufficiently interested in the Last Post and who were prepared to make the daily commitment required, but the question of integration – musical and otherwise – with the older generation also had to be considered.

In 1977, at the instigation of Dr. Caenepeel, an essay competition on the subject of the Last Post was organised in conjunction with the secondary schools in Ypres.

The first weekend in September 1977 also saw an important triple anniversary: the 60th anniversary of the Third Battle of Ypres and the 50th anniversary of both the inauguration of the Menin Gate and the foundation of the Last Post. In addition to a special Last Post ceremony, the celebrations included a tattoo on the Market Square and a "British Night" in the Cloth Hall. On the same evening, two of the older buglers were presented with the M.B.E. (Member of the British Empire) in recognition of their dedicated service throughout many years. Relations between the Committee and the city authorities were back on track, thanks in part to a substantial increase in the city's subsidy. On 14 June 1979 the Last Post was played in the presence of the King and Queen of Belgium and attendance at the normal ceremony also continued to rise, as the decade drew to a close.

From 1 May 1981, the buglers were required to wear a blue blazer (with Last Post badge) every Sunday. This same "uniform" was also to be worn daily during the months of July and August. The financial situation of the Last Post Committee began gradually to improve: annual interest on an investment fund in Canada (set up by Canadian veterans in British Columbia) increased each year; regular income was still received from stamp issues; in 1982 a Mrs. Gladys Smith of New York bequeathed BEF 20,000 to the Committee. The only cloud on the horizon was the failure to attract new members: the membership figure remained static at between 100 and 150 for a number of years. Another black spot was a further "incident", which occurred following a Last Post ceremony attended by the Ambassador of South Africa at the beginning of 1982: several anti-apartheid protesters used the occasion to make a noisy political demonstration against the Johannesburg regime.

At a meeting with the city authorities in 1983, the Last Post Committee emphasised that it was important to avoid the ceremony degenerating into a mere tourist attraction. It was – and must remain – an act of homage. With this aim in mind, it was agreed to try and limit the number of ceremonies taking place at hours other than 8 o'clock in the evening. The city authorities were also involved in the organisation of a new essay competition for the local schools, to promote youth awareness of the Last Post, but the competition was postponed at the request of the Committee. This was the height of the cruise missile crisis in Belgium and it was feared that the competition might provoke protest or unfavourable comment, in view of the "current multiplicity of movements for peace and against the missiles." It was intended to re-launch the initiative in September 1984 – with clear guidelines as to permissible content – but other matters resulted in a further postponement, this time until September 1985.

On 17 May 1985 Pope John-Paul II visited Ypres. He celebrated mass on the Market Square and took part in a special Last Post ceremony under the Menin Gate, where he prayed for world peace. This unique event yet again resulted in ever-higher attendance at the daily

Pope John-Paul II on the steps of the Menin Gate, *17 May 1985.*

148

ceremony and other V.I.P. visits also continued to increase. The Duke of Kent and Princess Alexandra also visited in 1985 and were followed a year later by Mother Theresa of Calcutta and Sir Bob Geldof of Band-Aid fame. In the meantime, the number of buglers had been increased to seven, allowing the ceremony to be played by three buglers per day (instead of the traditional two). The Last Post Committee was also accorded the status of a "protected" royal organisation in 1985.

A unique and inspiring ceremony (1985-...)

During the 1980's the interest of young people in the Last Post Ceremony once again began to grow. A number of them saw (and still see) the Last Post as a symbol of peace. The Last Post Committee was not wholly in agreement with such a standpoint: "The ceremony is an act of remembrance for those who died, in particular those who defended our country and our city. However, this act of remembrance can undoubtedly help to focus the thoughts of those present on the futility of war, which in turn can lead to a greater general desire for peace". During the annual general meeting on 11 May 1989 Chairman Guy Gruwez underlined that: "The ceremony is an act of remembrance and thanks. As such, its main focus must be on those who died. The implications of their deaths for the cause of peace are only a secondary consideration. There are many groups visiting the Menin Gate who place greater emphasis on the cause of peace than on the remembrance of the fallen, when it should be the other way around." In 1991 it was agreed that no activities or events should be organised within the framework of a Last Post ceremony that were not in keeping with the broad general spirit of the Committee's statutes. To avoid potential difficulties, all speeches were to be agreed in advance with the Committee, with a clear emphasis on the remembrance of the fallen.

The continuing increase in the number of visitors required the Committee to purchase a loudspeaker system for speeches during special ceremonies. At the same time, further attempts were made to restrict the number of these special ceremonies, particularly those not taking place at 8 o'clock. On 11 and 12 July 1987, the 70th anniversary of the Third Battle of

Ypres and the 60th anniversary of the inauguration of the Menin Gate were celebrated in the presence of Prince Filip of Belgium and Princess Alice, the Duchess of Gloucester. Later the same year the 20,000th Last Post took place.

Towards the end of the 1980's, the Committee once again went in search of "young blood", to ensure the continued future of the event. A number of suitable candidates were found and were gradually added to the Board of Directors.

At the beginning of the 1990's the Committee reached agreement with the city authorities on the thorny issues of crowd and traffic control at the Menin Gate. As a result, a number of bollards and chains were purchased. There was also a new information folder, with a revised text. Another suggestion was for the creation of a Last Post Band (including bag-pipers), which could be used at special ceremonial events. Sadly, this proposal – which did not originate from the Last Post Committee – ultimately came to nothing.

The number of requests for the playing of the Last Post at locations other than the Menin Gate also increased. These requests came principally from neighbouring towns, such as Langemark and Zonnebeke, but occasionally there were ceremonies performed in Northern France. Somewhat further afield, in November 1997 (the year of the 80th anniversary of the Third Battle of Ypres) Chairman Guy Gruwez and three of the buglers were invited by the Australian government to tour in Australia. Last Posts were played in Brisbane, Sydney, Melbourne and Perth. The highlight of the visit came on Remembrance Day, when the buglers played at the Australian War Memorial in Canberra – the new home of the lions that once stood at the old Menin Gate in Ypres.[150]

On 12 July 1992, during the commemoration of the 75th anniversary of the Third Battle of Ypres and the 65th anniversary of the inauguration of the Menin Gate, six new silver bugles were presented to the Last Post Committee. Two further bugles were presented on ANZAC Day 1997 by George O'Brien of Mudgeeraba, Queensland (Australia).

On 11 November 1998, on the occasion of the 80th anniversary of the end of the First World War, the Last Post ceremony was attended by King Albert II and Queen Paola of Belgium and by Queen Elizabeth II of Great Britain. Many other civil and military dignitaries were also present and the event was broadcast live by both British and Belgian television. The following year ex-President George Bush Snr.of the United States was also present under the Menin Gate. By the end of the 1990's, the Last Post was attracting over 200,000 visitors per year – more than ever before.

In 1999 the Last Post Committee formally amended its name to the Last Post Association. Its task, however, remained the same: to ensure that the Last Post continues to be played "for ever" at the Menin Gate, so that the ceremony can be held at least once in honour of every single soldier who died.

The signatures of Queen Elizabeth II, King Albert II and Queen Paola in the City of Ypres Book of Honour, *11 November 1998.*

After more than 75 years, the Last Post continues to be a unique and inspiring daily event. Moreover, this inspirational quality is not only evident from the writings of poets and authors. In November 1996, Jim Garrahy and Linda Kay Bell from Gettysburg (U.S.A.) attended the Menin Gate ceremony. So impressed were they by what they saw and heard, that they decided to launch a similar event in their hometown, the scene in July 1862 of one of the bloodiest battles during the American Civil War. "Taps" – the American equivalent of the Last Post – is now regularly played at the entrance to the American National Cemetery in Gettysburg.

The Last Post has many imitators in many other lands, but there is only one "true" Last Post – and that is the Last Post sounded each evening at 8 o'clock under the Menin Gate Memorial in Ypres. Since 1928, hundreds of thousands of people have heard and been moved by the haunting strains of those melancholy notes – none more so than the boarders in the adjacent St Vincentius College, who like many other nearby residents, have little option but to listen to the ceremony every night.

Like the Menin Gate itself, the Last Post Ceremony is open to numerous different interpretations. Some see the ceremony as being too overtly patriotic and militarist. Others regards it as a terrible warning of the dangers of war. Still others see it as a symbol of peace, a call to the nations of the world to settle their differences amicably. The organisers themselves see it as a mark of respect to those who died in defence of the city.

Whatever the merits of these various opinions, the Last Post has become an integral part of daily life in Ypres. The melody – which on some evenings is carried by the wind across the entire city – reminds both local people and visitors of the terrible sufferings endured by Ypres during the Great War and by the hundreds of thousands of young men who died here. Without the Menin Gate and without the Last Post Ceremony, Ypres would be a different – and a poorer – place.

Notes

[1] The Cloth Hall and Bell Tower, together with a number of other Flemish belfrys, are now listed by Unesco as "world heritage" buildings.

[2] STYNEN (H.). 'Opvattingen over het herstel van de hal te Ieper', in *Wonen/TABK*, maart 1983, 4-5, p. 32-43.

[3] For the discussions concerning the possible rebuilding of Ypres, see:
BAILLEUL (J.-M.), *Problematiek omtrent de wederopbouw van België na de Eerste Wereldoorlog, casus Ieper en omgeving (1918-1924)*. Ghent, unpublished thesis, 1976.
DE NAEYER (A.), 'La reconstruction des monuments et des sites en Belgique après la première guerre mondiale', in *Monumentum*, 1982, XX-XXI-XXII, p. 167-188.
STYNEN (H.), CHARLIER (G.) and BEULLENS (A.), *15/18 Het Verwoeste Gewest. Mission Dhuicque*. Brussels, Monumenten- en Landschapszorg & Bruges, Marc Van de Wiele, 1985.
STYNEN (H.) and DUVOSQUEL (J.-M.), *Omtrent de vestingstad Ieper*. Brussels, Koning Boudewijnstichting and Gemeentekrediet, 1992.
Verwoest Gewe(e)st. Ieper 1919-... De wederopbouw van een stad en een streek, visitors' guide for an exhibition in the Municipal Museum in Ypres, 1 May - 14 November 1999.

[4] BECKLES WILLSON, *In the Ypres Salient. The story of a fortnight's Canadian fighting, June 2-16, 1916*. London, Simpkin, Marshall, Hamilton, Kent & Co, 1916, p. 13.

[5] BECKLES WILLSON. *Ypres, the holy ground of British arms*. Bruges, Beyaert & London, B.T. Batsford, 1920, p. 1-2.

[6] Archives of the Royal Palace in Brussels, manuscript of speech by Albert I on 19 May 1920.

[7] For the history of this organisation: WARE (F.), *The Immortal Heritage. An account of the Work and Policy of the Imperial War Graves Commission during twenty years 1917-1937*. Cambridge, University Press, 1937.
LONGWORTH (Ph.), *The Unending Vigil. A history of the Commonwealth War Graves Commission 1917-1967*. London, Constable, 1967.

[8] Archives CWGC, WG 272: 8th Meeting IWGC, 21 January 1919.

[9] Archives CWGC, WG 360, part 1: Ypres. General File, 1919-1923.

[10] Ibidem.

[11] Public Record Office (PRO), WO/32/5853.

[12] There were already three cemeteries near the Minneplein (behind the prision – what is now Ypres Reservoir Cemetery).

[13] Archives CWGC, WG 360, part 1: Ypres. General File, 1919-1923 & General State Archives (ARA) Brussels, Dienst der Verwoeste Gewesten, 14647: Ypres - conservation des ruines, 1919-1921.

[14] Archives CWGC, WG 546, part 1: Anglo-French Mixed Committee, 1st meeting & general.

[15] Beckles Willson was born in Montreal on 26 August 1869 and until the Great War worked as a journalist in Canada and Great Britain (*Daily Mail*, 1896-

1898). During the war he served in the Canadian Expeditionary Force. He was in the Ypres Salient during the fighting at Mount Sorrel in June 1916. From 1917 onwards he was Inspector of War Trophies, first on the Western Front and later in Palestine. After his promotion to lieutenant-colonel, Beckles Willson was made Town Major of Ypres. In the 1920's and 1930's he founded two organisations: the Ypres League in 1920 and the Anti-Noise League in 1933. In between, he spent a number of years in colonial serive in West Africa. He died at Beaulieu (France) on 18 September 1942. His publications include novels, poems, biographies (George III, James Wolfe, Lord Strathcona), historical works (*The Hudson's Bay Company, The East India Company*) and essays (*Occultism and common sense, England by an overseas Englishman, Monetary Essays*). Source: *Who Was Who*.

[16] BECKLES WILLSON, *Ypres, the holy ground of British arms*. Bruges, Beyaert & London, B.T. Batsford, 1920, p. XIII.

[17] DELAERE (C.), 'Oorlogsdagboek deel II (9 mei 1915-1920)' in GELDHOF (J.)(Ed.). *Oorlogsdagboeken over Ieper (1914-1915)*, tweede deel. Bruges, Genootschap voor Geschiedenis, 1977.

[18] BECKLES WILLSON, *From Quebec to Piccadilly and other places. Some Anglo-Canadian Memories*. London, Jonathan Cape, 1929, p. 301-302.

[19] Archives CWGC, WG 360, part 1: Ypres - General File, Feb. 1919 - Dec. 1923. & BECKLES WILLSON, *From Quebec to Piccadilly and other places*, p. 330.

[20] ARA, Dienst der Verwoeste Gewesten, 14647: Ypres - conservation des ruines, 1919-1921.

[21] BECKLES WILLSON, *From Quebec to Piccadilly and other places*, p. 305.

[22] BECKLES WILLSON, *From Quebec to Piccadilly and other places*, p. 300 & *Ottawa Citizen*, 20 April 1919. Cutting in: ARA, Dienst der Verwoeste Gewesten, 14385: Sépultures militaries & monuments commémoratifs, 1919-1922.

[23] ARA, Dienst der Verwoeste Gewesten, 14647: Ypres - conservation des ruines, 1919-1921 and Archives CWGC, WG 360, part 1: Ypres - General File, Feb. 1919 - Dec. 1923; WG 1617: National Battlefields Memorials Committee; WG 277/2: Battle Exploits Memorials Committee - Minutes of Meetings; WG 857: Battle Exploit Memorials - Dominions - General File.
      BECKLES WILLSON, *From Quebec to Piccadilly and other places*, p. 300-333.

[24] ARA, Dienst der Verwoeste Gewesten, 14647: Ypres - conservation des ruines, 1919-1921 and Archives CWGC, WG 360, part 1: Ypres - General File, Feb. 1919 - Dec. 1923; WG 277/2: Battle Exploits Memorials Committee - Minutes of Meetings.

[25] Archives CWGC, WG 360, part 1: Ypres - General file, Feb. 1919 - Dec. 1923.

[26] City Archives Ypres (SAI), Ypres acquisitions, temporary no. M18.

[27] Archives CWGC, WG 360, part1: Ypres - general file, Feb. 1919 - Dec. 1923.

[28] Ramparts Cemetery (Lille Gate).

[29] Archives CWGC, WG 360, part 1: Ypres - general file, Feb. 1919 - Dec. 1923.

[30] Archives CWGC, SDC 61: Transactions of Sir Frederic Kenyon, Letter from Blomfield to Kenyon, 18 August 1919.

[31] Archives CWGC, Add 2/1/1: Battlefield Memorials - memorandum by the Secretary of State for War, 19 November 1919.

[32] Archives CWGC, WG 277/2 Battle Exploits Memorials Committee Minutes of

Meetings, Report of Sir Reginald Blomfield, R.A., on the National Memorial at Ypres, 25 September 1919.

[33]   Archives CWGC, WG 360, part1: Ypres - general file, Feb. 1919 - Dec. 1923; Add 2/1/1: Battlefield Memorials - memorandum by the Secretary of State for War, 1919-1921; WG 1617: National Battlefields Memorials Committee; WG 277/2: Battle Exploits Memorials Committee - Minutes of Meetings, 1919-1921.

[34]   Hansard (*Parliamentary Debates, Commons*), 5th series, 1910-1925 (3/11/1919, 13/11/1919, 9/12/1919); Archives CWGC, WG 360, part 1: Ypres - general file, Febr. 1919 - Dec. 1923.

[35]   PRO, WO/32/5569.

[36]   *Le XXe Siècle*, 29 January 1920 (cutting in ARA, Dienst der Verwoeste Gewesten, 14647: Ypres - conservation des ruines, 1919-1921).

[37]   Foreword by Capt. James LEE, Town Major of Ypres, in MAGRATH C.J., *Ypres-Yper. A few notes on its history before the war - with a plan of the town*. London, YMCA, 1918, p. 3.

[38]   Cutting in ARA, Dienst der Verwoeste Gewesten, 14647: Ypres - conservation des ruines, 1919-1921.

[39]   Archives CWGC, WG 360, part 1: Ypres - general file, Febr. 1919 - Dec. 1923.

[40]   Archives CWGC, WG 360, part 1: Ypres - general file, Febr. 1919 - Dec. 1923; WG 1617: National Battlefields Memorials Committee & ARA, Dienst der Verwoeste Gewesten, 14647: Ypres - conservation des ruines, 1919-1921.

[41]   In a number of Flemish cities, displaced citizens of Ypres formed "Ypres clubs" add weight to their demands.

[42]   ARA, Dienst der Verwoeste Gewesten, 14647: Ypres - conservation des ruines, 1919-1921 & Archives CWGC, WG 360, part 1: Ypres - general file, Febr. 1919 - Dec. 1923.
BAILLEUL (J.-M.), *Problematiek omtrent de wederopbouw van België na de Eerste Wereldoorlog, casus Ieper en omgeving (1918-1924)*. Ghent, unpublished thesis, 1976.
BAILLEUL (J.M.), 'Recht op herstel?' in BAERT (K.) e.a., *Ieper, de herrezen stad.* Koksijde, De Klaproos, 1999, p. 21-66.

[43]   Archives CWGC, WG 360, part 1: Ypres - general file, Febr. 1919 - Dec. 1923.

[44]   ARA, Dienst der Verwoeste Gewesten, 14647: Ypres - conservation des ruines, 1919-1921.

[45]   PRO, CAB 21/219: "Conclusions of a conference held on 5th July 1920 at 12 noon".

[46]   Hansard (*Parliamentary debates, Commons*), 5th series, 28 October 1920 & PRO, WO/32/5569.

[47]   PRO, CAB 21/219: "Cabinet. Finance Committee. Memorandum by the First Commissioner of Works, 13 December 1920".

[48]   PRO, CAB 21/219: Stamfordham (personal secretary to King George V) to Hankey (secretary of the Cabinet), 15 December 1920.

[49]   Archives CWGC, WG 360, part 1: Ypres - general file, Febr. 1919 - Dec. 1923.

[50]   ARA, Dienst der Verwoeste Gewesten, 14647: Ypres - conservation des ruines, 1919-1921.

[51]   Archives CWGC, WG 1617, National Battlefields Memorial Committee: Report of the National Battlefields Memorial Committee, 24 February 1921.

[52] ARA, Dienst der Verwoeste Gewesten, 14647: Ypres - conservation des ruines, 1919-1921.

[53] Ibidem.

[54] Cutting in Archives CWGC, WG 219/2/1, part 3: Memorials to the missing - Tyne Cot & Menin Gate, part 3.

[55] Archives CWGC, WG 1617, National Battlefields Memorials Committee: report, 21 February 1921.

[56] Archives CWGC, WG 360, part 1: Ypres - general file, report 21 January 1921.

[57] Archives CWGC, WG 1617, National Battlefields Memorials Committee.

[58] Archives CWGC, WG 219/2/1, part 1: Memorials to the missing - Tyne Cot & Menin Gate, letter by Ware to Ingpen, 4 May 1921.

[59] Archives CWGC, WG 219/2/1/7 Menin Gate Unveiling, part 1: Note by Chettle, Director of Works, 14 Juin 1926, & WG 219/2/1, part 1, passim.

[60] Archives CWGC, WG 1617, National Battlefields Memorials Comittee: letter from Ingpen to Ware, 12 October 1921.

[61] Archives CWGC, WG 1687/1 Cabinet Advisory Committee on the Memorials to the Missing, report by Blomfield, 21 November 1921.

[62] Archives CWGC, WG 1687/2 Cabinet Advisory Committee on the Memorials to the missing - proceedings of subcommittee appointed in connection with IWGC memorial at Ypres.

[63] Archives CWGC, WG 219/2/1/2, part 1: Memorials to the missing Menin Gate - Contract & Construction, reports by Blomfield, 21 March 1922 & 31 May 1922.

[64] Archives CWGC, WG 219/2/1/3 Sir R. Blomfield's agreement for the Menin Gate, 26 January 1922 - 28 January 1926.

[65] BLOMFIELD (R.), *Memoirs of an architect*. London, Macmillan, 1932, p. 187.

[66] Archives CWGC, ADD 1/1/19 Fabian Ware re: inscriptions Menin Gate.

[67] Archives CWGC, WG 219/2/1, Memorials to the Missing Tyne Cot & Menin Gate, part 2: report by Blomfield to the Director of Works of the IWGC, s.d.

[68] Archives CWGC, WG 219/2/1/2, part 2: Memorial to Missing Menin Gate & Tyne Cot - Contract & construction, from March 1926 on; WG 219/2/1/2, part 3: Contract for the construction of the Memorial to the Missing Menin Gate & WG 219/2/1/4.

[69] Archives CWGC, WG 219/2/1, Memorials to the Missing Tyne Cot & Menin Gate, part 2 (January 1924).

[70] Archives CWGC, WG 219/2/1/7 Menin Gate Unveiling part 1: Letter from Ingpen to Ware, 18 May 1927.

[71] Archives CWGC, WG 219/2/1/7 Memorial to Missing - Menin Gate unveiling part 2, from July 1927: "A note on the Menin Gate" by Blomfield, July 1927.

[72] Cutting in Archives CWGC, WG 219/2/1, part 3: Memorials to the Missing - Tyne Cot & Menin Gate Part 3. An English translation can be found in BLOMFIELD (R.), *Memoirs of an architect*, p. 190-191.

[73] BLOMFIELD (R.), *French architecture and its relation to modern practice*. The Zahanoff Lecture 1927. Oxford, Claredon Press, 1927, p. 21.

[74] BLOMFIELD (R.), *Memoirs of an architect*, p. 179.

[75] Archives CWGC, WG 219/2/1 Memorials to the Missing - Tyne Cot & Menin Gate Part 2: Letter from Blomfield to Ware, 10 October 1927.

[76] VANDEMAELE (S.), *Britse oorlogskerkhoven en monumenten voor de gesneuvelden van 1914-1918 in Noord-Frankrijk en West-Vlaanderen.* Ghent, unpublished post-graduate thesis, 1986, p. 73.

[77] BLOMFIELD (R.), *Memoirs of an architect*, p. 188.

[78] Ibidem, p. 189.

[79] GRANVILLE FELL (H.), *Reid Dick.* London, Tirant's, 1945, p. v.

[80] BLOMFIELD (R.), *Memoirs of an architect*, p. 187.

[81] Archives CWGC, ADD 1/1/19 Fabian Ware.

[82] BLOMFIELD (R.), *Memoirs of an architect*, p. 189.

[83] GRANVILLE FELL (H.), *Reid Dick*, p. xi.

[84] BLOMFIELD (R.), *Memoirs of an architect*, p. 191.

[85] *Omtrent de vestingstad Ieper.* Brussels, Gemeentekrediet - Koning Boudewijn-stichting, 1992, passim and CORNILLIE (J.E.), Ieper door de eeuwen heen. Langemark, 1950, passim.

[86] DE BRUYNE (T.), 'Ieperse leeuwen in het verre Canberra' in *Shrapnel*, February 1998, p. 50-55.

[87] A summary of which is to be found in BURNESS (E.), 'The Menin Gate Lions' in Sabretache vol. XXIX, April-June 1988, p. 10-19.

[88] Based on: Archives CWGC, WG 219/2/1/7 Menin Gate Unveiling - Part 1 & WG 219/2/1/7 Menin Gate Unveiling - part 2, from July 1927 onwards and *Het Ypersche/La Région d'Ypres*, July-August 1927.

[89] BLOMFIELD (R.), *Memoirs of an architect*, p. 187.

[90] Oil on canvas, 140,5 op 271,8 cm, Australian War Memorial, Art 9807.

[91] FRY (G.) & QRAY (A.), *Masterpieces of the Australian War Memorial.* Canberra, 1982, p. 110 & 137.

[92] *"Menin Gate at Midnight" (Or "The Ghosts of the Menin Gate"). The story of Captain Will Longstaff's Great Allegorical Painting.* s.l., s.d., s.p.

[93] Archives CWGC, WG 219/2/1/16 Painting Longstaff.

[94] REID (R.), *He is not missing. He is here! Australians and the Menin Gate. Visit to Australia by buglers from the Menin Gate*, Ypres Belgium 1-15 November 1997. Canberra, Department of Veterans'Affairs, 1997, p. 61.

[95] Archives CWGC, WG 219/2/1, part 2 Memorials to the Missing - Tyne Cot & Menin Gate, Aug. 1928.

[96] Ibidem: Letter from Blomfield to Ware, 10 October 1927.

[97] Archives CWGC, WG 219/2/1, part 3 Memorials to the Missing - Tyne Cot & Menin Gate, Aug. 1928 - Dec. 1936.

[98] Ibidem.

[99] Quoted by Admiral Jellicoe in the foreword to T*he Story of an Epic Pilgrimage. A Souvenir of the Battlefields Pilgrimage of 1928.* London, British Legion, 1928, p. 7.

[100] Archives CWGC, WG 219/2 Memorials to the missing - practical.

[101] LONGWORTH (Ph.), *The unending vigil.* London, CWGC, 1967, p. 105.

[102] Archives CWGC, WG 219/2/1, part 3: Memorials to the Missing Tyne Cot & Menin Gate, August 1928 - December 1936.

[103] During the 1950's about 120 German cemeteries were "concentrated". The remains were transfered to the present-day cemeteries in Langemark, Menen and Vladslo. This explains the huge numbers of casualties buried in German cemeteries: more than 44,000 in Langemark and almost 48,000 in Menen. Tyne

Cot Cemetery, the largest British military cemetery in the world, contains "only" 12,000 burials

[104] QUAGHEBEUR (R.), *'t Westland in oorlogstijd*. Veurne, De Klaproos, 1995, p. 39-42 and 58-61.

[105] In Flanders Fields Document Centre, Menin Gate documents, Hand-written notes by Dr. Alfred Caenepeel.

[106] Archives CWGC, WG 219/2/1, part 3: Memorials to the Missing Tyne Cot & Menin Gate, August 1928 - December 1936, letter from Blomfield to Ware d.d. 24 December 1940.

[107] SAI, 547.5: Menenpoort - oorlogsschade 1940.

[108] SAI, 547.5: Oorlogsschade Engelse kerkhoven en monument.

[109] STANLEY J. Blenkinsop in *The Daily Mail*, 14 August 2001.

[110] The Germans only destroyed the war monuments they considered to be offensive to the German nation. Around Ypres this included the monument to the first gas attack at Steenstrate, the monument to the Queen Victoria Rifles at Hill 60 and the texts of certain demarcation stones.

[111] BOURGEOIS (H.), 'Hitler et la région de Comines-Warneton en 1914-1918 et en 1940' in *Mémoires de la Société d'Histoire de Comines-Warneton et de la Région*, Tôme XVII, 1987, p. 381-438.

[112] Quoted in DE LAUNAY (J.), *Hitler en Belgique*. Strombeek-Bever, Byblos, 1975, p. 80.

[113] QUAGHEBEUR (R.) and VERBEKE (R.V.), *Ze zijn daar!* Veurne, De Klaproos, 1994, passim.

[114] WOOLLCOMBE (R.), *Lion Rampant. The 15th Scottish Division. Normandy to the Elbe*. London, Leo Cooper, 1970, p. 125.

[115] WINGFIELD (R.M.), *Een Tommy in de Lage Landen*. Utrecht/Antwerpen, Prisma-boeken, 1955, p. 130.

[116] Archives CWGC, WG 219/2/1, part 5: Memorials to the Missing Tyne Cot & Menin Gate (re-opening of Commission's work and subsequent correspondence).

[117] Archives CWGC, WG 219/2/1, part 2.

[118] Conversation with Maurice Baratto, August 2001.

[119] Archives CWGC, WG 219/2/1, part 5.

[120] The description is taken largely from: JACOBS (M.), *Zij, die vielen als helden... Inventaris van de oorlogsgedenktekens van de twee wereldoorlogen in West-Vlaanderen*, deel 2. Bruges, Province of West Flanders, 1996, p. 141-142.

[121] Archives CWGC, WG 219, part 3: Revised Procedure.

[122] Archives CWGC, WG 219/2/1 Lists.

[123] Archives CWGC, WG 219/2/1/15 Menin Gate - Additional names.

[124] Archives CWGC, WG 219/2/1 Lists.

[125] VERBEKE (R.V.), 'De Menenpoort in Ieper: een gedenksteen voor vermisten' in *Shrapnel. WFA-Magazine*, Year 1997, nr. 2, p. 23-29.

[126] Unless otherwise stated, the contents of this section are based on the "Registre des Proces-Verbaux" of the Last Post Committee, the minutes of the association from 1930 to 1992. With thanks to Guy Gruwez, chairman of the Last Post Association

[127] Archives CWGC, F 868/1/1/5 Sounding of Last Post: letter from Coleman to Ware, d.d. 10 July 1928.

[128] Archives CWGC, SDC 42 Menin Gate and Ware, press clipping.

[129] *Het Ypersche*, 6 oktober 1928.

[130] Archives CWGC, WG 219/2/1, part 3 Memorials to the Missing - Tyne Cot & Menin Gate Aug. 1928 - Dec. 1936, letters from Perrott, Higinson and Ducrôt, November 1928.

[131] *Het Ypersche*, 21 September 1929.

[132] The Ypres Last Post Committee should not be confused with the Canadian Last Post Fund. This Fund was set up before the First World War and helps to undertake the maintenance of military graves in Canada.

[133] "Last Post Committee à Ypres" à Ypres - Association sans but lucratif. Statuts. (Copie in extenso de l'acte n°705 publié aux annexes au Moniteur belge du 30-31 mai 1930). Bruxelles, Imprimerie du Moniteur belge, 1930, s.p.

[134] Archives CWGC, WG 219/2/17 Last Post 1930-1934.

[135] Archives CWGC, F 868/1/1/5, part 1: Menin Gate Sounding of Last Post.

[136] Archives CWGC, WG 219/2/1, part 3 Memorials to the Missing - Tyne Cot & Menin Gate, Aug 1928 - Dec 1936 & *Het Ypersche*, 19 oktober 1935.

[137] Archives CWGC, F 868/1/1/5, part 1: Menin Gate Sounding of Last Post.

[138] *The Times*, 8 October 1936.

[139] Archives CWGC, F 868/1/1/5, part 1: Menin Gate Sounding of Last Post.

[140] Joseph Arfeuille (Ypres, 11 October 1897 - 16 January 1971), known as Fred, was a well-known Ypres figure. He was a wood-cutter by trade and also one of the earliest Last Post buglers. In addition, from 1938 to 1970 he was the official city "jester", one of whose tasks was to throw replica cats from the Bell Tower during the famous Cats Festival. Arfeuille was well-known for his partiality to the fruit of the vine - and of the hop.

[141] Archives CWGC, F 868/1/1/5, part 1: Menin Gate Sounding of Last Post, report Juin 1946.

[142] Archives CWGC, WG 219/2/1, part 5: Re-opening of Commission's work and subsequent correspondence.

[143] *'t Ypersch Weekblad*, 29 October 1944.

[144] Archives CWGC, F 868/1/1/5, part 1: Menin Gate Sounding of Last Post, report d.d. 28 July 1955.

[145] *The Yorkshire Post*, 14 March 1959 and 17 March 1959.

[146] Published in the Belgisch Staatsblad (State Gazette) on 14 April 1960, p. 623.

[147] Archives CWGC, F 868/1/1/5, part 2, Sounding of Last Post, 1963.

[148] Archives CWGC, F 868/1/1/5, part 1: Menin Gate Sounding of Last Post.

[149] Archives CWGC, WG 360/4, part 11: Ypres Memorial Church and School.

[150] [REID R.], *He is not missing. He is here!*, p. 6.

[151] Ibidem, p. 9.

[152] BUSHAWAY (B.), *The Great War and Remembrance*. In PORTER (R.) (Ed.), *Myths of the English*. London, Polity Press, 1992, p. 146.

Acknowledgements

This book could not have been written without the valued assistance of Richard Kellaway, Director-General of the Commonwealth War Graves Commission, Peter Francis and Shirley Hitchcock of the Commonwealth War Graves Commission in Maidenhead, Christine Connerty-Ketels of the Commonwealth War Graves Commission in Ypres, Guy Gruwez OBE, AOM and Ian Connerty of the Last Post Association, Director Stephen N. Gower of the Australian War Memorial, Lady Patsy Alliot and Anthony Beckles Willson, Maurice Baratto MBE, Jan Claus, Joan Collick, Madelon Dendooven, Lieutenant-Colonel Ludo Meulebroucke, Rik Opsommer, Julian Putkowski, Frans Pyck, Guido Vanbeselaere, Roger Verbeke, my colleagues in the In Flanders Fields Museum (Piet Chielens, Jan Dewilde, Annick Vandenbilcke, Diederik Vandenbilcke, Roos Wildemeerch) and Katelijne Vanbeselaere.